Finding Your Ministry

Finding Your Ministry

A Study of the Fruit and Gifts of the Spirit

by

Raymond W. Hurn

with

Albert L. Truesdale ● Mildred Bangs Wynkoop
Morris A. Weigelt ● Paul R. Orjala

Beacon Hill Press of Kansas City
Kansas City, Missouri

ISBN: 0-8341-0609-4

Printed in the
United States of America

Permission to quote from the following copyrighted versions of the Bible is gratefully acknowledged:

The *New American Standard Bible* (NASB), © The Lockman Foundation, 1960, 1962, 1968, 1971, 1972, 1973, 1975.

The Holy Bible, New International Version (NIV), copyright © 1978 by the New York International Bible Society.

The *Revised Standard Version of the Bible* (RSV), copyrighted 1946, 1952, © 1971, 1973.

Unless otherwise indicated, all scripture references are from the *New International Version.*

15   14   13   12   11

Contents

Foreword

Another book on spiritual gifts? Yes, But here is a book that is different. It has a clearly defined goal stated by Dr. Raymond W. Hurn, executive director of the Department of Home Missions:

1. To look at ourselves—the Church, the Body of Christ.
2. To look at the harvest.
3. To look at our work force.

Finding Your Ministry is both theoretical and practical. Scriptural and theological positions are examined, expounded, and explained by scholars Dr. Albert Truesdale, Jr., Dr. Mildred Bangs Wynkoop, Dr. Morris Weigelt, and Dr. Paul R. Orjala. Dr. Hurn provides guidance which is focused on helping lay persons find "their ministry."

In this age of staggering spiritual need, it is our hope and prayer that a diligent study of this Christian Service Training text will provide insight and understanding of spiritual gifts so that members of the Church of the Nazarene may serve as an instrument of blessing and healing to the full limit of their God-given abilities.

GEORGE COULTER

Preface

The spiritual gifts emphasis is an integral part of the church growth study material widely used throughout the church. In the denomination-wide study of church growth sponsored by the Department of Home Missions (*Get Ready to Grow*, 1978), Dr. Paul Orjala presents an introduction to the subject of spiritual gifts. Dr. W. T. Purkiser has also written an excellent and scholarly treatment on the gifts of the Spirit. The *Diagnostic Clinic* material examines the church body, its possible diseases, its community setting, its growth, and especially its deployment of workers. Spiritual gifts understanding and development is a logical next step in growth realization.

Inasmuch as some religious groups have so greatly dramatized language and sign gifts, many in the conservative tradition have simply not spoken out affirmatively and positively on this issue of spiritual gifts.

It has been my intention to put the gifts of the Spirit in proper perspective and not to leave our faithful members in a vacuum of misunderstanding.

In these pursuits I have been greatly aided by a symposium of our finest scholars elected by a large group of Nazarene scholars meeting in June, 1978. Among them are Drs. Paul Orjala, Mildred Wynkoop, Morris Weigelt, Frank Carver, Rob Staples, Irving W. Laird, Paul Bassett, Don Owens, Bill Sullivan, and Alex Deasley. These and a number of additional scholars have advised, counseled, and in many ways helped me in regard to the total under-standing of church growth in the Nazarene biblical-theo-logical context.

Church growth focuses in some depth on the sociologi-cal principles that produce growth. These include the homogeneous principle (a tool for targeting on special groups), soil testing, nonreceptive and receptive peoples, primary groups, goals ownership, and many other subjects. (See Paul Orjala's book *Get Ready to Grow.*)

There are biblical and spiritual principles that are basic to the growth of the Body of Christ. It would be wrong to leave the impression that church growth principles deal only with the sociological.

It is now our purpose to explore these biblical princi-ples in some depth. We have drawn especially on theolo-gians and biblical scholars (Drs. Truesdale, Wynkoop, Weigelt, and Orjala) for special assistance in writing key chapters.

The study of spiritual gifts is being set in the context of each one "finding his or her own ministry in the Body of Christ." We trust that this brief study will both enlighten and inspire all of us to a more fruitful and effective church-manship as we go about fulfilling the Great Commission "to make disciples" (cf. Matt. 28:19-20).

—RAYMOND W. HURN

1

GOD'S WORD:
Our Guide to Spiritual Gifts

By Raymond W. Hurn

Twice recently in the middle of the night I was jarred into sudden wakefulness with a powerful illumination of my mind and heart concerning the work of the Holy Spirit. In those moments of sudden awakening from deep sleep, key Scripture passages came to my mind with fresh reminders of how God the Holy Spirit is effectually at work in the hearts and minds of those who are His children.

> We have different gifts, according to the grace given us *(Rom. 12:6)*.

> It was he who gave some to be apostles . . . prophets . . . evangelists . . . pastors . . . teachers, to prepare God's people for works of service, so that the body of Christ may be built up until we all reach unity in the faith and in the knowledge of the Son of God and become mature, attaining the full measure of perfection found in Christ.

> Then we will no longer be infants, tossed back and forth by the waves, and blown here and there by every wind of teaching and by the cunning and craftiness of men in their deceitful scheming. Instead, speaking the

truth in love, we will in all things grow up into him who is the Head, that is, Christ. From him the whole body, joined and held together by every supporting ligament, grows and builds itself up in love, as each part does its work *(Eph. 4:11-16).*

I have been crucified with Christ and I no longer live, but Christ lives in me *(Gal. 2:20).*

Now about spiritual gifts, brothers, I do not want you to be ignorant. . . . There are different kinds of spiritual gifts, but the same Spirit. There are different kinds of service, but the same Lord *(1 Cor. 12:1, 4-5).*

These awakenings and Scripture reminders have been all the more impressive to me because of the deep and abiding concern which I have for the Church of the Nazarene as a religious movement in these latter days.*

I believe that holiness churches are destined to play a key role in evangelizing contemporary society. Our heritage has prepared us for this particular time. The Wesleyan doctrines dear to holiness people are especially in harmony with spiritual advance. This should make a big difference in the way we live, the way we relate to each other in the Body of Christ, and in the mission which God calls us to perform. But has this always been true in actual practice? I'm afraid not. No system always works perfectly at all times.

Our Wesleyan theological tradition began with John Wesley in England in the late 1700s. But John Wesley was himself the inheritor of a tradition that came to him in an unbroken line of holiness teaching from the New Testa-

---

*This concern has guided and motivated me in developing a process of church growth training participated in by 90 percent of our district superintendents, 5 of our 6 general superintendents, 35 of our best scholars, and 700 of our district church growth committeemen. This first step led to the denomination-wide CST study *Get Ready to Grow* (1978), where many thousands of others were led through a process of understanding the mission of the Church of Jesus Christ in the context of the modern church growth movement.

ment Church itself. How this tradition was preserved and projected through the centuries is admirably documented by Dr. William Greathouse in *From the Apostles to Wesley*.[1] The doctrine of the Holy Spirit is not a new thing; it has been an explicit part of Christian heritage from the Day of Pentecost.

Now, when the attention of the Christian world is freshly focused on the relationship between spiritual gifts and church growth, holiness people can be contemporary simply by being what we are. Spiritual gifts have been with us all along as described in the pages of the Holy Bible.

PRACTICAL IGNORANCE

Some of us have been in practical ignorance of spiritual gifts—a condition that Paul warned about when he wrote, "Now about spiritual gifts, brothers, I do not want you to be ignorant" (1 Cor. 12:1). This practical ignorance, which some have translated "agnostic," has limited our life and our ministry.

It is no credit to the Christian church in general that we have left the young in a vacuum of understanding of biblical truth. As a result we have witnessed a rapid growth of cults in our society. We do need to understand who we are and the biblical basis for any position we take. We need not remain in practical ignorance of spiritual gifts; indeed, we must turn again and again to the inspired Word of God to guide us in this delicate and important area of our ministry to the Body of Christ.

Central to our understanding of spiritual gifts is the fact that the gifts of the Holy Spirit are "gifts of grace." They come from God for the purposes of God. The Holy Spirit is himself the Gift of the risen Christ and is thereby the means by which Christ continuously imparts graces or

13

gifts to His followers according to the needs of His Body the Church.

In his classic little book *The Gifts of the Spirit*, Dr. W. T. Purkiser says, "Nothing is more important in practical Christian service than the recognition and use of the gifts of the Spirit."[2]

The New Testament, Dr. Purkiser notes, "has a special word for spiritual gifts. It is *charismata*." For the Greeks, the root word *charis* meant "grace." The New Testament writers used *charis* to describe, in Dr. Purkiser's words,

> the spontaneous, beautiful, unearned love of God at work in Christ Jesus. Stemming from *charis, charisma* is a singular noun that literally means "grace gift." It stands for any of the spiritual endowments that Christians have in varying degree and form. This is of course a far cry from the popular use of *charisma* to describe the glamor, winsomeness, or personal magnetisim of some popular political figure or star of stage or screen.[3]

Study of Spiritual Gifts Is Important

There are benefits in the study of spiritual gifts for ourselves, but there are also benefits to be derived in the Body of Christ, the Church. As we study spiritual gifts, we should develop stronger unity within the Body, understanding how to work together in greater harmony.

Because of the widespread use of the *Spiritual Gifts Workshop,* we have been able to get multiplied numbers of survey results from those who participated. The almost universal testimony has been that these workshops on spiritual gifts have gone far to relieve guilt, to help Christians to "think soberly" about themselves and to be released to move forward in the power of the Spirit to a more meaningful development of the gifts that God has so clearly bestowed. Some have testified that a study of spiritual gifts has revealed weaknesses as well as strengths in spiritual life, especially as they have put themselves under the judgment of the local body to confirm or not to confirm certain spiritual gifts.

Donald Guy of Kaneohe, Hawaii, has for a period of more than two years used spiritual gifts as a primary yardstick in church responsibility assignments. Such assignments are made after first looking at the qualifications of individuals based on apparent endowment with spiritual gifts. "The result has been a greater response to needs and greater responsibility after accepting assignments. Board meetings average more than 95 percent in attendance and a spirit of harmony and trust prevails."

The Roseburg, Ore., church has for many years made spiritual gifts teaching and implementation a part of the discipling and development process. The growth of this church from 186 members to 501 members in nine years in itself speaks volumes about the methods that they have used. It is true that the study and development of spiritual gifts in a congregation brings to the fore some abuses and weaknesses which must be overcome, but the overriding result has been responsible, productive church body life development.

From the East Coast one Nazarene testified that his spiritual gift mix was intercession, faith, and hospitality, and that when the body confirmed these spiritual gifts, it "gave me a special awareness that I have a responsibility to use these gifts for Christ's glory. It definitely helped me!" This person testified also that the first indication that he had certain spiritual gifts was when he saw the scores recorded on paper; God's will opened up in a new way. He said, "Then God took over!"

Several pastors have spoken of the personal enrichment when one section of the Body confirmed a spiritual gifts mix of prophet, teacher, pastor, shepherd, and/or

15

administration. Confirmation helped "in the realization of a measure of success."

In looking through the survey forms from the *Spiritual Gifts Workshops,* I have yet to discover any individual who reports that the confirmation of spiritual gifts had hindered him. In every case the report has come back that having spiritual gifts confirmed has encouraged or helped each one. Others expressed ideas to the effect that discovery of spiritual gifts had helped to develop their ministry, or helped them to be at peace, or had given them confidence in the exercise of Christian responsibilities.

KEEPING THE GOAL IN MIND

What is the goal of this study? Indeed, what is the goal of our church? Exegesis has been developed by some of our best scholars on the nature of the Church and spiritual gifts for this study. We will all be the better for having experienced this. But what is the main goal to keep in mind? Our goal is contained in the Great Commission which Christ gave to His Church.

> "Therefore go and make disciples of all nations, baptizing them in the name of the Father and of the Son and of the Holy Spirit, and teaching them to obey everything I have commanded you. And surely I will be with you always, to the very end of the age" *(Matt. 28:19-20).*

The goal is to make disciples. The Great Commission contains action verbs. Three are helping verbs but one, "to make disciples," is an imperative.

Let us not be content in any church unless we are making "disciples." If we are not making disciples, there is all the more need that we look with keen evaluation in three directions.

1. First, we need to take a look at ourselves—this part of the Church, the Body of Christ. This ought not to be too

hard for us to do in this day when self-improvement books and study courses are multiplied a thousandfold on every newsstand. We ought to be as wise as worldly people concerning secular success. Some may find this difficult to do, however, for we are not accustomed to giving and receiving feedback from one another in an objective mode. We are often "hung up" over focusing on people—their differentness—instead of focusing our attention on ideas and principles. We then become critical of persons, develop faulty communications, and retard personal growth.

Some of our churches are sick, based on their performance in winning disciples. Diagnostic clinics have provided a self-discovery tool that assists a local church in finding the possible diseases that may be encountered.* But not all are sick. We don't have to be sick to find better concepts and better methods.

2. We need to take a look at the harvest. How much of it is there? How responsive is the harvest? Jesus commanded us to look at the harvest. He talked a great deal about putting seed in responsive soil. Many thousands of Anglos, people like the most of us in the North American church, are awaiting an invitation, according to 1978 Gallup poll results.**

---

*The *Diagnostic Clinic* can be purchased from the Nazarene Publishing House and has an instrument in it that pinpoints the weaknesses or the disease within a church that is plateaued or declining. Preventive measures are always good even in churches of good health.

**Some results from the 1978 *Unchurched American Survey* conducted by Dr. George C. Gallup for a consortium of religious bodies including the Church of the Nazarene:

61 million Americans are not members of any church or religious institution.

Of these—

76 percent say they sometimes pray to God.

74 percent want their children to receive religious instruction.

68 percent believe in the resurrection of Jesus Christ.

52 percent would be open to an invitation to attend church.

Pastor Don Wilkins and his church in Grand Rapids, Mich., looked at the harvest and discovered large numbers of Spanish-speaking people and American Indians nearby that were not being ministered to.

Historic Los Angeles First Church has been looking at its harvest fields and discovered that although many Anglo members have now moved to the suburbs or gone to heaven, large numbers of Korean and Spanish people now surround the church and are being ministered to in language congregations in addition to the English-speaking service. Recently they discovered Southeast Asian harvest fields little known previously. These are people from Thailand, Cambodia, Burma, Vietnam, and other Southeast Asian countries. They discovered that the Thais operate businesses within a three-mile radius of Los Angeles First Church that includes 37 restaurants, 6 grocery stores, 7 beauty salons, and 4 travel agencies. The heart of Thai town is only three-fourths of a mile north of First Church.

Proclamation of the holiness message has begun through Thai translation. They plan home Bible study programs, gospel literature and gospel tape distribution. Once a month they plan for simultaneous translation of the worship service in several different languages that all of these congregations of people might join together in worship and praise to God.

The New England District, like New York, Florida, Chicago, and many more, has been looking on its harvest fields. District Superintendent William Taylor reports a population mix of Asians, Blacks, and Spanish. Recently immigration quotas allowed a great influx of Cape Verdean Portuguese. The district has imported a successful pastor from Brazil, and now his son is also helping in this harvest.

The Oregon Pacific District has been looking on its harvest fields and decided to start 80 to 100 churches immediately. Thirty pastors were installed in the summer of

1979 to launch new work. The three churches of Eugene joined in sponsorship of 20 new churches in and around their city of 185,000. They were motivated by the harvest. Jesus said not to wait. "Look at the fields! They are ripe for harvest" (John 4:35).

3. We must also take a look at our work force. How are the people of the church being discipled? How are they being trained? How are they being deployed to reach our goal of discipling large numbers of people? Denver First Church has led the way in a great discipling program that is having a ripple effect throughout the denomination. Our Youth Department has developed excellent materials in discipleship for young Christians which may be ordered from the Nazarene Publishing House.

Many of our churches have recently gone through the entire church growth cycle in an effort to deploy more greatly a work force of trained, discipled people for the harvest. The denomination-wide study of *Get Ready to Grow* may have been followed by a Diagnostic Clinic or a Spiritual Gifts Workshop. Many report that God is breaking through, souls are being saved, and the work is growing. We believe God is pleased when we enter into the harvest of souls to make disciples.

Is There Biblical Support for Nongrowth?

Is there a biblical basis for nongrowth? We do not know of any. On the other hand, a biblical basis for rapid growth can certainly be supported. (Read Acts 2:47; 6:1.) Lukewarm or lethargic churches are decried (Rev. 3:14-16). Study Christ's teaching on the harvest. How is the church to grow? There is no way that it can grow except through the members of the Body of Christ. We have rested too long in the medieval concept of the church as being a location or a building. Sometime, somewhere, I believe we will have a congregation of dozens of house churches drawn from many aspects of life (not from just one homogeneous unit) with many bivocational leaders . . . discipling . . . teaching . . . winning souls to Christ, coming together perhaps once each week for celebration or for protracted meetings held in large rented halls.

It is not pleasing to God that a church should plateau as soon as they have 24 to 35 members or at the 65 to 74 level. I envision the doubling of at least 2,500 of our churches in the next decade, and that is far too conservative! I can see through the eye of faith the multiplication of churches on such a scale that 1,900 new ones could be created within the next 10 years in the United States, Canada, and Britain alone.

If we have a museum mentality, this will not happen. Preoccupation with maintenance-motivated concepts may help us to sing sedately, "Precious memories, how they linger . . ." while the church is quietly dying. A fortress mentality will lead us to depend on loyalty to traditions, but this will not win the young, especially if the goals are set by old-timers who bypass the current generation.

We can see the great growth which we long for if we are responsive to the biblical mandate to go and make disciples. Diversification is the true sign of life, not unification. In this study we hope to discover the many, many ways that Christ gifts His people for service. Can we be united in our diversity? The compulsion to "freeze" the situation or to make all the "decisions" may indicate a fortress mentality.

We will want to approach this study prayerfully and with the Bible in hand. Begin now to familiarize yourself with 1 Pet. 4:10-11; Ephesians 3 and 4; Galatians 5; Romans 12; and 1 Corinthians 12. Read the passages in several versions. The *New American Standard Bible* and the *New International Version* are particularly helpful and reliable.

THE GIFTS LIST

A simple listing of gifts mentioned in the Scripture includes the following from the *New American Standard Bible.* (Perhaps you should compare this version with the King James, the *New International Version,* or other versions.)

Ephesians 4	apostles
	prophets
	evangelists
	pastors
	teachers
Romans 12	prophesying
	serving
	teaching
	exhortation
	giving
	leading
	showing mercy
1 Corinthians 12	wisdom
	knowledge
	faith
	healing
	miracles
	prophecy
	distinguishing of spirits
	tongues (languages)
	interpretation of tongues
	(languages)

Which Gifts Are Yours?

Aren't you a little curious about which of the spiritual gifts are yours? Usually each person will find a mix of spiritual gifts with two or more of the gifts operational through their personality. Often you will find different gifts operational at a particular point in your life. These may not have been of high visibility to you and the church at an earlier time. Early in my ministry, I felt that I had a special gift or anointing as a young evangelist. When I preached, people often came to the altar seeking help from God. Early in my career I evidenced administrative or organizational gifts, though I was not aware of it at the time. I thought of myself as a shepherd/pastor, a counselor, an encourager; but later, administrative gifts seemed to rise more and more to the fore. Now I view myself as a facilitator to help other people to succeed in their spiritual and soul-winning endeavors. Administrative gifts have been more and more confirmed by the Body and I get great joy from influencing, facilitating, and conceptualizing in planning meetings to help others to know how to succeed best.

What are your spiritual gifts? Why don't we find out? We have designed a simple, self-examination that will help you affirm possible areas of gifting. It's not a surefire method, but it might help prepare you for the study that is ahead if you were to take a simple spiritual gifts test. You may be surprised at how high you score in certain areas. You will probably discover high scores in more than one area, as it is usually true that each person operates with a "gift mix."

Whether you can clearly define a spiritual gift operational in your life or not, you certainly can define some functions that are necessary to the success of God's work. Perhaps you are not involved in a function such as teacher, usher, singer, accountant, nursery or parking attendant. It may be that part of the Body is confirming some special gift that God has given you for your role.

Let us be careful that we do not allow abuses or distortions to arise as a result of this study. We will talk about some of these abuses later. A word of caution is important as we begin. No human test is absolutely certain to determine a spiritual gift. No man-made approach is "surefire." We do hope to stimulate you to thought, prayer, and study that you may find your very own ministry in the kingdom of God where you will serve with success and feel good about yourself and about the church as you serve.

FINDING GOD'S WILL

Our prayer and desire is that we may be led to discover God's will for our lives. Dr. C. Peter Wagner reminds us in his book that ignorance is not bliss. He says, "Ignorance of spiritual gifts may be a chief cause of retarded church growth today. It also may be at the root of much of the discouragement, insecurity, frustration and guilt that plagues many Christian individuals and curtails their total effectiveness for God."[4]

SOME THINGS TO DO

This first session, let us use the following exercise to determine where our strongest possibilities lie in spiritual gifts.

SCORING INSTRUCTIONS

1. Answer 20 questions in the six categories A, B, C, D, E, F. Score yourself 0 if you do not experience the particu-

lar statement in your own life. Score yourself as high as 5 if the statement in each category represents a high degree of intensity or frequency of the experience. If it is not a real high degree of intensity or frequency, you may want to score yourself with a 2, 3, or 4. Be practical and pragmatic with each question.

2. Record the score in each column on the Score Sheet. If you do not understand the process, ask help from your instructor.

3. When you have answered each question, total the score on each line, showing the total score for A, B, C, D, E, and F in the appropriate place.

4. Circle the three highest total scores. Put a check mark beside the next three highest scores.

5. When you have finished, check the key in the Appendix (or that provided by the instructor) to write in the spiritual gift in the blanks numbered 1 through 20.

6. Now meet in small groups of four or five to talk about the way you have scored yourself. Ask other members of the church how they feel about the way you have scored yourself.

Sample of Score Sheet

Spiritual Gifts	A	B	C	D	E	F	Total Score	Indicated Gifts
1. _____	5	3	3	4	3	2	(20)	
2. _____	3	3	2	2	3	2	15	
3. _____	2	2	3	3	3	4	17	
4. _____								
5. _____								
6. _____								
7. _____								

SCORE SHEET

SPIRITUAL GIFTS PROFILE

Spiritual Gifts	A	B	C	D	E	F	Total Score	Indicated Gift
1.	4	5	5	5	4	5	28	PROPHECY
2.	5.	5	5	5	3	5	28	SERVING
3.	5	5	5	5	5	5	30	HELPING
4.	3	5	5	5	4	5	27	TEACHING
5.	3	5	0	0	0	0	8	ENCOURAGE
6.	5	0	0	0	5	3	13	GIVING
7.	5	5	1	2	0	5	18	LEADERSHIP
8.	5	5	5	5	5	5	30	COMPASSION
9.	5	5	4	0	4	5	23	PASTOR
10.	4	0	0	5	1	0	10	APOSTLE
11.	5	0	3	1	3	0	12	MISSIONARY
12.	5	3	0	0	3	0	11	EVANGELIST
13.	5	5	2	0	0	5	17	WISDOM
14.	5	5	3	2	5	5	25	KNOWLEDGE
15.	4	3	0	5	0	5	17	DISCERNMENT
16.	0	5	0	0	0	3	8	HEALING
17.	0	3	0	0	0	5	8	MIRACLES
18.	0	0	0	0	0	5	5	FAITH
19.	0	0	0	0	0	0	0	LANGUAGES
20.	0	0	0	0	0	0	0	INTERPRETATION

Spiritual Gifts Profile—Schedule A

1. God has given me understanding about the future.
2. I understand the importance of keeping rooms tidy and comfortable.
3. I am able to carry out special assignments for other Christians.
4. I can explain Bible facts in such a way that people's lives are changed.
5. I can persuade others toward self-improvement even if they are at first reluctant.
6. My giving to God's work easily surpasses 10 percent of my income.
7. I can take full responsibility for my decisions with no excuses.
8. I can think of ways to make life easier for those in physical distress.
9. I am able to empathize with others.
10. I can take responsibility for groups of Christians in many different communities.
11. I can readily adjust to a culture different from my own.
12. I can explain clearly the meaning of salvation from the Bible.
13. I can usually select a course of action which benefits other Christians.
14. I am able to remember facts.
15. The people I vote for usually make good officers.
16. I enjoy praying for the healing of sick persons.
17. In the name of the Lord I have done the otherwise impossible.
18. Through prayer, God has let me know in advance that a certain person would be saved.
19. I can write or speak in more than one language.

20. I can quickly grasp different shades of meaning in a language other than my native tongue.

Spiritual Gifts Profile—Schedule B

1. I feel satisfaction in giving God's Word to a group.
2. I enjoy helping others to be comfortable.
3. I like to run errands for other Christians.
4. I enjoy learning new things.
5. I like to advise others for their benefit.
6. I consistently make money far above a salaried person's income.
7. I enjoy making decisions affecting the course my church will take.
8. I enjoy doing little things for people who are unable to take care of themselves.
9. I enjoy helping other Christians to grow spiritually.
10. I welcome the responsibility for the spiritual growth of large numbers of people.
11. I can learn from others who have a life-style radically different from my own.
12. I enjoy turning secular conversations to spiritual matters.
13. I enjoy seeking knowledge for life's problems and applying it.
14. I like to learn about how God has acted in human history.
15. It interests me to look for the reason why people say or do things.
16. I entertain no doubts but that God does heal miraculously in these days.
17. It does not bother me to risk my reputation for God's Word.

18. When circumstances seem to contradict God's Word, I still find it easy to trust in God, and that faith usually is rewarded.
19. God has helped me to witness in a second language.
20. God has helped me to understand a second language.

Spiritual Gifts Profile—Schedule C

1. God's blessing seems to attend my presentation of biblical messages and these are received well by the people.
2. People come up and thank me for little things I do around the church.
3. I am asked to do things which require skill but which receive little public recognition.
4. People ask me for information about the Bible or other bodies of knowledge.
5. I have been a big help to others in making a decision to do something for the Lord.
6. My income is large enough to allow me to contribute large sums to Christian colleges, churches, or charities.
7. Other Christians seek my opinion and follow my suggestions.
8. I am asked to visit persons with special needs such as the elderly or handicapped.
9. People express appreciation for the spiritual help they have received through our friendship.
10. I have been authorized by my church to lead other Christians or to begin new churches in official capacities.
11. I know immediately if I am embarrassing other people by my words or acts.
12. I have power in prayer and have carried a burden in audible prayer until prayer was answered.

13. People seem inclined to accept my advice and act upon it.
14. I have been asked to do specific study projects in the Bible.
15. People in authority ask my opinion about giving certain jobs to certain people.
16. People who are sick ask me to visit and pray with them.
17. People have told me that I have more faith in the possibility of miracles than they do.
18. Other Christians have commented on how much I seem to trust in God.
19. I find that audiences are responsive when I speak to them in their own language when it is not my native tongue.
20. I have been asked to interpret for a speaker in another language.

Spiritual Gifts Profile—Schedule D

1. When I reveal what I feel is God's will, others seem willing to follow.
2. I enjoy doing routine jobs around the church such as arranging chairs, tables, hymnals, and so on.
3. When someone else is in charge, I can think of ways to help him/her succeed.
4. When I teach, people learn.
5. When lonely people are known to me, I easily converse with them and they seem to be helped.
6. When special financial needs in the church are brought to my attention, I can draw upon reserve funds to help meet that need.
7. My decisions carry weight with other Christians.

8. When told of another's misfortune, I know what kind of aid is required.
9. People under my influence grow spiritually.
10. I understand the biblical and denominational traditions to be transmitted to a new generation.
11. I can establish meaningful communication with people of other nationalities.
12. When I tell how Christ saved me, others see their need for a Savior and are converted.
13. I can help other people find Christian solutions to their moral and spiritual problems.
14. I am able to get fresh insights from what I learn.
15. I can tell the difference between genuine spirituality and its imitation.
16. I have prayed for the healing of another person and healing has resulted.
17. I have seen the laws of nature altered because of my prayers.
18. God has given me promises which later actually came true.
19. People who speak other languages understand me readily.
20. I can think in two languages simultaneously.

Spiritual Gifts Profile—Schedule E

1. I have been asked by fellow Christians to express God's Word in group situations.
2. I am asked to do common tasks that others don't want to do.
3. Pastors, Sunday school leaders, and other persons in authority feel comfortable in asking me to help them.

4. I can find different methods to explain the same truths.

5. When friends and fellow members feel depressed, they like for me to visit them.

6. I rejoice in giving large amounts even as I did when my income was less.

7. I have been elected to carry out key responsibilities involving decision-making.

8. People remember that I was helpful to them during their illness, even for a long time afterwards.

9. People confide their problems to me.

10. I have been elected to serve the church on the district or general levels.

11. People of other cultures trust me and react pleasantly and with meaning to me.

12. People have told me that I seem sensitive to their problems or spiritual condition.

13. People often come to me for help in deciding on a course of action for their lives.

14. People have commented on my knowledge of the Bible.

15. I have effectively dealt with problems related to the occult, demon possession, etc.

16. God answers my prayers for healing in a way visible to others.

17. I am often given unusually difficult tasks because people know that God is with me to believe for miracles.

18. People have called me a man/woman of faith.

19. I have been asked to write letters for people in a language different from my own.

20. People ask me to explain what someone else meant, especially when the other person speaking is of a different age or culture.

Spiritual Gifts Profile—Schedule F

1. If I were to receive clear understanding of God's will, I would not hesitate to make His will known to others.
2. I am able to do routine jobs without sacrificing attention to detail.
3. I can be content when someone else gets the credit for what I have done.
4. I can see myself teaching a Sunday school class or a home Bible study group.
5. It is not hard for me to listen to those who are confused or distressed and to help them put forth their best efforts.
6. I would be content with a financially simpler life-style than I have at present, if that would advance Christ's kingdom.
7. I would like to see others follow my guidance in God's work.
8. I feel a sense of confidence that I can help ill or bereaved persons.
9. I would not mind helping someone who needed to talk over a problem, even if it interrupted my rest.
10. I enjoy the thought that God might use me in a significant way to other nationalities.
11. I accept differentness in people without judgment.
12. I would not be afraid to seek out unbelievers in order to witness to them about Christ.
13. I understand how biblical truths can be lived out in life.
14. Learning new truths from the Bible is exciting to me.
15. I can distinguish between right and wrong.
16. I have a sense of confidence that through prayers of faith I can help someone who is injured or ill to get better.

17. I have great confidence in the miracle-working power of God.
18. "God says so" is all the proof I need that something will happen.
19. I can express complex thoughts in simple language.
20. I can understand complicated ideas and repeat them accurately in simpler words.

FOR ADDITIONAL READING

Greathouse, William. *From the Apostles to Wesley.* Kansas City: Beacon Hill Press of Kansas City, 1979.

Orjala, Paul. *Get Ready to Grow.* Kansas City: Beacon Hill Press of Kansas City, 1978.

Purkiser, W. T. *The Gifts of the Spirit.* Kansas City: Beacon Hill Press of Kansas City, 1975.

Schaller, Lyle. *Understanding Tomorrow.* Nashville: Abingdon Press, 1976.

Wagner, C. Peter. *Your Spiritual Gifts Can Help Your Church Grow.* Glendale, Calif.: Regal Books, 1979.

2

EPHESIANS:
The Church Is Christ's Body

By Albert Truesdale, Jr.

GOD IS AT WORK!

It is obvious to many people that God the Holy Spirit is today at work in the Church, renewing, teaching, and commissioning it. Evidences of His renewing presence may be seen in all denominations. Surely all Christians rejoice over this renewal of the Church and the awakening awareness among Christians of the possibilities of grace and responsibilities of discipleship.

Renewed interest in the gifts of the Holy Spirit is a vital part of what the Holy Spirit is doing in the Church. Along with this renewed interest comes the responsibility to understand the Holy Spirit's activity.

The Church of the Nazarene has tried to safeguard the Spirit's free activity and creativity in the Church; at the same time we have insisted that what is understood to be the activity of the Holy Spirit be submitted to scrutiny by the Bible.

THE CHURCH: THE BODY AND FULLNESS OF CHRIST

All of us know how important it is to begin at the right place if we expect to arrive at the desired goal. A dressmaker doesn't begin by sewing buttons onto uncut cloth; an automobile mechanic doesn't begin to change the oil in a car by pouring the new oil into the crankcase. Where one starts does make a difference, and it is no less true in matters of Christian faith.

Discussion of the Church begins properly with the person and work of Jesus Christ. Quite simply, the Church is the creation of Jesus Christ through the Holy Spirit.

> For he chose us in him before the creation of the world to be holy and blameless in his sight *(Eph. 1:4)*.
> And you also were included in Christ when you heard the word of truth, the gospel of your salvation. In him, when you believed, you were marked with a seal, the promised Holy Spirit *(Eph. 1:13)*.
> And God placed all things under his [Christ's] feet and appointed him to be head over everything for the church, which is his body, the fullness of him who fills everything in every way *(Eph. 1:22-23)*.

The Church exists primarily not by human activity but by the redemption accomplished by Christ in His life, death, resurrection, and ascension.

He is Lord of the Church, and to none other does the Church owe its life or give its allegiance.

> And he is the head of the body, the church; he is the beginning and the firstborn from among the dead, so that in everything he might have the supremacy *(Col. 1:18)*.

He is its Head and this place He shares with no one else (as we saw in Eph. 1:22-23). Everything that God does in the Church—its creation, redemption, worship, and servanthood ministry to the world—is directly provided by the atoning work of Jesus Christ.

> [Jesus Christ] gave himself for us to redeem us from all wickedness and to purify for himself a people that are his very own, eager to do what is good *(Titus 2:14)*.

Who Is This Christ?

But let us be sure who this Christ is. He is God incarnate in Jesus of Nazareth. In Jesus we do not meet a half God and half man. Rather, in Him we encounter the Eternal God who became incarnate, enfleshed, in Jesus of Nazareth who was himself fully man. We confess Him to be God's Christ. In Him God has fully disclosed himself in human history as the Creator. Therefore, since the One who is the Head of the Church is the One in whom we meet the Creator/Redeemer God, we see that the Church is indeed a creation of God's grace, through the Son, and by the activity of the Holy Spirit. Furthermore, in the Church the glory of God as Creator and Redeemer is to be displayed. It is a holy temple of the Lord (Eph. 2:21).

The Church is called into existence by the resurrected Lord and *His presence constitutes its fellowship.*

Christ creates the Church and calls you and me to life in it. He *is* the Church's life, and you and I have His life where the resurrected Lord makes himself known in the Church "which is his body, the fullness of him who fills everything in every way" (Eph. 1:23). When I realize that I share the redemptive presence of Christ through my brothers and sisters in the Lord, then my life as a contributing and receiving member of the Church takes on an entirely different significance. But it is really only through such an understanding that the New Testament language about the Body of Christ and about ministry within the Body of Christ makes any sense at all.

36

The Church, then, is a creation of grace. It is the direct creation of the gospel, which means "good news." But what is the gospel? The gospel is the Good News that while we were yet sinners, Christ died for us, the ungodly (Rom. 5:8). It is the proclamation that God has not dealt with us according to our sins but has freely extended forgiveness and reconciliation to all who will turn from their sin and live only in the new life He offers. The gospel is indeed a *new reality*. Through the atonement of Christ the old order of death, guilt, and destruction has passed away, and all things have become new (2 Cor. 5:17). To as many as will receive Him, John said, to them He gives the power to become "the sons of God" (John 1:12). And Paul says that in Christ God reconciles the world to himself.

> God was reconciling the world to himself in Christ, not counting men's sins against them. And he has committed to us the message of reconciliation *(2 Cor. 5:19)*.

The Church is intended to be a gospel community. In it the Good News is celebrated through the life of its members. In it the power of God unto salvation is brought to realization and demonstration. The Church is indeed "a happening," the event/place where He who is the Word of God is present as the resurrected Lord, giving himself to its members, and they to Him, and both to the world as the Good News.

THE HOLY SPIRIT AND THE CHURCH
JOHN 14—15

Now we need to ask, "What is the relationship of the Holy Spirit to Christ and to the Church?"

Perhaps the best place to begin is with Jesus' instructions to the disciples in John, chapters 14 and 15. In chapter 15 Jesus says that the Holy Spirit will bear witness in the Church and in the world that Jesus is indeed the Christ.

> "When the Counselor comes, whom I will send to you from the Father, the Spirit of truth who goes out from the Father, he will testify about me" *(John 15:26)*.

He testifies not about himself but about Christ. Everything He does—comforting the Church, teaching, and convicting the world concerning sin and righteousness—will point to the Lordship of Christ. All that the Holy Spirit does in the Church and in the individual believer will bring glory to the Lord who alone made atonement for sin and who is alone Head of the Church. The glory of the Holy Spirit in the Church and the world is to bear witness that in Jesus of Nazareth the righteousness of God has appeared unto salvation, that He is the Christ of God. To this end all of the Holy Spirit's activities are directed. Any doctrine of the Holy Spirit that separates Him from the atonement of Christ and His primacy in the Church must be rejected as injurious to its life and mission.

The Holy Spirit's confession that Christ is Lord must not be seen simply as a verbal statement. For Him to bear witness and to bring us to confess that Christ is Lord means that He becomes Lord and Redeemer in every quarter of our lives. Through the Holy Spirit the resurrected Christ is made fully redemptive in the Church and in the world. Through His work, who Christ *is* becomes synonymous with what He *does:* Creative Redeemer (John 1:1-5, 9-14).

NEVER APART FROM CHRIST

The Holy Spirit does nothing in the Church or the world apart from the person and work of Christ. He always exalts the One who was crucified and raised to life again; He always points men and women to Christ and makes Him present in the Church. Therefore whenever we speak of the fruit of the Spirit, or of the gifts of the Spirit, we are talking about the Lordship of Christ being demonstrated through the ministry of the Holy Spirit.

Christians must never allow the work of the Holy Spirit to drift away from the person and work of Christ. The Holy Spirit never supersedes the reconciliation made on the Cross by God in Christ between himself and the world. Where the Holy Spirit is at work, He bears witness to Christ who is "far above all rule and authority, power and dominion, and every title that can be given, not only in the present age but also in the one to come" (Eph. 1:21).

So the Church is the creation of Christ through the Holy Spirit. Through His witness we know that the Son is in the Father, that we are in the Son, and that He is in us.

THE PROPER WORK OF THE HOLY SPIRIT

The Holy Spirit will always act to fulfill among men what God in Christ accomplished in the Cross and the Resurrection, namely, to reconcile the world to himself through holy love and to transform them into His own image.

> Do not conform any longer to the pattern of this world, but be transformed by the renewing of your mind. Then you will be able to test and approve what God's will is—his good, pleasing and perfect will *(Rom. 12:2).*

This also means that through the power of God's reconciling deed in Christ, the Holy Spirit seeks to reconcile men and women to themselves and to their neighbors. And He does this by casting out the sin and guilt that causes alienation between God and man and among people, and by re-creating them in holiness and in love. The

Holy Spirit creates community, and the Church is to be God's demonstration before men of what true human existence and community can be.

> Be shepherds of God's flock that is under your care, serving as overseers—not because you must, but because you are willing, as God wants you to be; not greedy for money, but eager to serve; not lording it over those entrusted to you, but being examples to the flock *(1 Pet. 5:2-3).*

The Wesleyan Genius

The genius of the Wesleyan doctrine of the Holy Spirit is that (1) it safeguards the relationship of the Holy Spirit to Christ; (2) it understands that the work of the Holy Spirit is to effect in the process of history what the atonement of Christ made possible—reconciliation, holy love toward God and man, and the re-creation of community among men; and (3) that the presence of the Holy Spirit in the believer will be evidenced not by fabulous manifestations, but by the fruit of true holiness—"love, joy, peace, patience, kindness, goodness, faithfulness, gentleness and self-control" (Gal. 5:22-23).

Unity in Diversity

Before turning to the relationship of the fruit and gifts of the Spirit, let us look first at the unity and diversity of the Church as described in Ephesians, chapter 4. The Church is often described as a unity in diversity, and this seems to be an appropriate description of Paul's discussion in this chapter of Scripture. The Church is one, not because of a single governmental structure or some other human evidence, but because Christ is one and the Church is one in Him as its Lord and Head. The Church has no meaning apart from His presence that gives it life. He is the Church's life; He is its unity. And the Holy Spirit cultivates this unity in all that He does.

Therefore, Paul says, there is only one body and one Spirit that enlivens the body. There is only one hope, that we are reconciled to God through Christ by faith alone and await His return in honor and glory. There is only one Lord, one faith, one baptism into Christ; and "one God and Father of all, who is over all and through all and in all" (Eph. 4:6).

Nothing that subverts this unity can be of God. Party strife, self-seeking, and such things do not evidence the Holy Spirit but are more properly characteristic of the fruits and works of the flesh or of the old life dominated by sin.

THE DIVERSITY OF CHRIST'S BODY

There is a diversity within the unity that enriches the Body of Christ. Paul's use of the body metaphor in 1 Corinthians and in Ephesians makes this clear. The Body of Christ is not a dull repetition of only one member. All the diverse members with their various functions are important to its life. No member is superfluous. Even though some members of the human body may be more attractive than others, their functions may be less significant for the body's well-being.

So in the Church the degree of visible exposure to attention is not the sole or chief criterion of significance or legitimacy for the members of Christ's Body. The central point made by Paul is that rather than frustrate unity, proper diversity enhances it. There is much more harmony and richness displayed in the integration of the parts into a whole than is present where monotony reigns and diversity is lacking.

But the diversity of the Church is fulfilled, not in

isolation by the parts, but in their integration into the whole Body, and indeed, into Christ, the Head of the Body, who gives coordination and meaning to the parts. The various parts of the Body of Christ are many ministries and many servants to each other and to the Head. For example, the foot finds fulfillment only as it serves the whole Body, and so on throughout the Body. Furthermore, if one part suffers, the whole Body does so as well. (Read all of 1 Cor. 12:26.)

The diversity of the Body of Christ, according to Eph. 4:13, finds its fulfillment not in itself, but in its Head who is Christ. The Body is "built up," enhanced, fulfilled, only when the fullness of Christ is realized in it. Because of His quickening presence, the Church achieves ever greater coordination among its members. Its "knowledge" of the Head, the Son of God, leads to the sort of maturity that attains "the full measure of perfection found in Christ" (Eph. 4:12-13).

THE PRIMACY OF THE FRUIT OF THE SPIRIT

The *unity* and *diversity* of the Church is demonstrated in another way: the fruit and gifts of the Spirit. There is a unity, a commonality in the Body, that marks the foot as a proper part of the Body. It is not, Paul says in 1 Corinthians, that the foot must look like the hand, but that both the foot and the hand evidence the unity that derives from the Head. The unity of the Church, and that which identifies the parts as belonging to the Head, is not one or several of the diverse parts, but the distinctive character —the life—of Him who is the Head of the Body.

Therefore the distinguishing evidence that Christ is in His Body, that the Body belongs to Him, will be that which is most characteristic of himself: *holy love.* This is exactly what Paul says in the 13th chapter of 1 Corinthians, for none of the diversities about which the Corinthians boasted had any significance apart from love. God *is* holy love, and His presence and work are characterized by *what He is*. He establishes the Church and the members in himself, and himself in them. Holy love that reconciles man to God and that reconciles people to themselves and to one another, is the evidence of the Holy Spirit's activity in the Church and in the world. And what the Holy Spirit is able to do in Christ's disciples is made possible through the life, death, resurrection, and ascension of Jesus who is the Christ. God was in Christ reconciling the world to himself.

ALL CHRISTIANS BEAR FRUIT

Now we are in a position to see the significance of the fruit of the Spirit. Let us notice first of all that the word is singular, "fruit," not "fruits" (Rom. 6:22, KJV; Gal. 5:22; Eph. 5:9; John 15:8). In each of these scriptures the Greek word *karpos*, "fruit," is singular. Although the fruit of the Spirit is manifest in a number of ways, it is one. And what is its oneness? The life of Jesus Christ being manifested in the Church and in its members. The fruit of the Spirit is the manifest life of Christ. And the life of Christ, as we have seen, establishes the Church and its members in the holiness and love of God.

Although we speak of the fruit of the Spirit, we should remember that in fact we are describing the fruit of Christ being realized in the Church through the work of the Holy Spirit. The Holy Spirit effects (or brings to pass) what the Church's Lord makes possible. The fruit of the Spirit is indeed the fruit of Christ.

The fruit of the Spirit—"love, joy, peace, patience, kindness, goodness, faithfulness, gentleness and self-control" (Gal. 5:22-23)—is made possible only through the redemption achieved by Christ in the Cross and Resurrection. These are not the results of self-discipline (although self-discipline is important), but of the transforming, redeeming, and sanctifying life of Christ in the Christian. The fruit of the Spirit, cultivated and maturing through the ministry of the Holy Spirit, is the evidence of Christ's life and the fullness of God's Spirit in the Christian.

Every person who is born of the Spirit, born again, will begin to bear the fruit of Christ's life because he or she is a new creation in Christ through the Spirit. Whereas in the old life our "members" were yielded to produce fruits of the flesh, now, by the enabling of the Spirit, our members are yielded (Rom. 6:13-14) to the Spirit to produce "a harvest of righteousness and peace" (Heb. 12:11). No born-again Christian lacks the fruit of the Spirit.

In John 15, Jesus says that the Father is glorified as the disciples bear fruit. We know that the production of fruit involves careful cultivation and time, and this is no less true of the Christian in whom Christ now lives as redeeming Lord.

The Spirit cultivates the life of Christ in the believer, and he who is born of God will earnestly desire to see Christ's life bear its proper fruit in every area of life. However, the Holy Spirit is at work in a human life that has come in contact with, and has been shaped by, many influences, some of which are quite contrary to the life of Christ in the believer. We should not be surprised to see the Holy Spirit working patiently and purposely to bring the whole person into harmony with the life of Christ that now characterizes the Christian. Jesus says that it is the work of the Father to trim the branches so that they can bear even more fruit.

> "I am the true vine and my Father is the gardener.
> He cuts off every branch in me that bears no fruit,

44

> while every branch that does bear fruit he trims clean
> so that it will be even more fruitful" *(John 15:1-2)*.

Every sincere Christian opens his entire existence to the fruit-producing activity of the Holy Spirit. Paul says in Romans, "Yield yourselves to God as men who have been brought from death to life, and your members to God as instruments of righteousness" (Rom. 6:13, RSV).

The New Testament is absolutely clear on this point: The *evidence* of the Holy Spirit in the life of the believer is to produce the fruit of Christ's life—holy love. This is the power of the gospel: God in Christ through the Holy Spirit succeeds in creating for himself a people in whom His own life—holy love—is the characterizing quality.

Gifts of the Spirit in the Church

Now we are ready to talk about the gifts of the Spirit in the Church. It is extremely important, as we have emphasized, to put all the elements of this discussion in their proper relationship to the overall understanding of Christ's work. To begin with, we need to realize that the gifts of the Spirit (as they are called in Heb. 2:4) are actually the gifts of Christ. Eph. 4:7 makes this clear: "But to each one of us grace has been given as Christ apportioned it."

It is the triumphant, resurrected Christ who gives diverse gifts to the Church. Verse 11 says that "it was he who gave some to be apostles, some to be prophets, some to be evangelists, and some to be pastors and teachers." But this does not exclude the work of the Holy Spirit who by the authority of Christ's atonement administers these gifts within the Body of Christ.

The next thing we learn is that the gifts of the Spirit are diverse. Consequently the plural form is used to describe them. They serve to achieve the proper diversity and ministry in Christ's Body described earlier. When understood in this light, they serve the unity of the Body, its coordination as an integrated, organic whole, where each part serves the well-being of the other.

The gifts of the Spirit serve the life of Christ in the Church, for they are means whereby the fullness of Christ's Body is achieved and evangelism engaged in. They are diverse, but they find their unity in the life of Christ.

GIFTS AND SERVANTHOOD

The gifts of the Spirit fulfill their purpose only when they appear as servants working to build up the Body of Christ (including its evangelizing function). They fail in their purpose any time they are used to promote the selfishness, pride, and egotism of one individual member, or whenever they lead to division within the Church. Paul makes it clear in Ephesians that the purpose of the gifts is "to prepare God's people for works of service, so that the body of Christ may be built up until we all reach unity in the faith and in the knowledge of the Son of God and become mature, attaining the full measure of perfection found in Christ" (Eph. 4:12-13).

Counterfeit gifts which are used for purposes of spiritual pride and discord must be rejected.

THE FRUIT OF HOLINESS

It should now be clear that no one gift to the Body can ever serve as *the* evidence of the Holy Spirit's presence and work. The true evidence of the Holy Spirit is that which is common to all members, the fruit of holiness. Furthermore, it should be evident that if the gifts are to serve their function, they too must be thoroughly characterized by that which is primary, that which is the fruit of the Spirit, *the fruit of holiness*. From the Early Church until today, many Christians go astray at this point. They improperly identify glamorous or spectacular occurrences as the truly substantial purpose of Christ's life, death, and resurrection. And they err grievously as a result. "For the kingdom of God is not a matter of eating and drinking, but of righteousness, peace and joy in the Holy Spirit" (Rom. 14:17).

This is why the Wesleyan tradition of which we are a part has stressed the doctrine of entire sanctification, of love made perfect through the work of the Holy Spirit, as essential to a full understanding of Christ's redemptive activity. We have realized, and quite correctly, that the principle and common mark of the Holy Spirit's presence is His *fruit,* the fruit which is indeed the life of the resurrected Lord in the Church.

The gifts of the Spirit are made by Christ to the Church and are given for the well-being of the Body. They are neither given as the private property of individuals, nor are they given in recognition of one's spiritual superiority. The gifts of the Holy Spirit are the "workhorses of the Church." They are servants in the Body, and they become perverted and destructive when understood otherwise. Without the love of Christ as their characterizing feature, they perish (1 Corinthians 13). "Instead, speaking the truth in love, we will in all things grow up into him who is the Head, that is, Christ" (Eph. 4:15). Through the gifts of the Spirit, the Church is enabled to become a servant community, servant not only to itself but also to the world.

A Mission of Redemption

The Church exists as mission as surely as fire exists by burning. In Jesus Christ God has acted to reconcile the whole world to himself. And the Church is the place where the power and truth of the new reality are realized and demonstrated. If the life of Christ characterizes the life of the Church, then it will have no other reason for existence than to become a redemptive community among men. There is no justification for its existence as a mutual admiration society, or to continue to exist just because it happens to be here. It exists as a mission of redemption. It lives and moves at the direction of its Lord. And the only way that the fruit and gifts of the Holy Spirit can fulfill their intended purpose is for the Church to bear authentic witness to the gracious, reconciling, and sanctifying reality that God has brought about in His Christ.

As a redemptive community, the Church needs to be faithfully engaged in following the Holy Spirit into the world, seeking to learn from Him new ways to realize the salvation of God among men. This is its responsibility and its joy! Today, the Holy Spirit is at work in the Church, teaching its members that we have not yet fully understood the possibilities of God's reconciling love among men.

Let this study in which we are engaged be free from the spiritual selfishness that concentrates on one's own well-being. Let it be an opportunity for us to see the comprehensive magnificence and mission of Christ's Church and our place in it. Let it be a time when we catch a new vision of the demands and possibilities of God's reconciling love.

Discussion Questions

1. Why is it important to start with the person and work of Christ in a discussion of the Church?

2. Why should the church be understood as an entire body rather than as a gathering of individuals?

3. What is the relationship between the Holy Spirit and the Lordship of Christ?

4. How does the Wesleyan tradition help us in comprehending the relationship of the Holy Spirit to Christ?

5. What are some ways that demonstrate the unity and diversity of the Church? How does Christ relate to the parts of the Church?

6. How does the presence of "holy love" affect the body of believers?

7. What is the significance of the fruit of the Spirit?

8. What is the meaning and the result of the gifts of the Spirit?

9. What does it mean to call the Church a "redemptive community"?

FOR ADDITIONAL READING

Carter, Charles Webb. *The Person and Ministry of the Holy Spirit: A Wesleyan Perspective.* Grand Rapids: Baker Book House, 1974.

Deal, William S. *Be Filled with the Spirit.* Kansas City: Beacon Hill Press of Kansas City, 1971.

Earle, Ralph. *The Quest of the Spirit.* Kansas City: Beacon Hill Press, 1951.

Gould, Joseph. *The Spirit's Ministry.* Kansas City: Nazarene Publishing House, 1941.

Greathouse, William M. *The Fullness of the Spirit.* Kansas City: Nazarene Publishing House, 1958.

Murray, Andrew. *Aids to Devotion, Thoughts on the Holy Spirit in the Epistle to the Ephesians.* London: Nisbet and Co., 1909.

Stedman, Ray C. *Body Life.* Glendale, Calif.: G/L Publications, 1977.

Steele, Daniel. *The Gospel of the Comforter.* Kansas City: Beacon Hill Press, 1960.

3

1 CORINTHIANS, GALATIANS:
God's Gifts Are for Reconciliation

By Mildred Bangs Wynkoop

Spiritual gifts are extensions from the Church, which is the Body of Christ, to the world for whom He died.

The gospel of Jesus Christ is the message which activates this extension. This message gives meaning to every part of the Body. No single part can be properly understood apart from this interrelationship.

The authority for the Christian Church is the Christian Book, the Bible. The blueprint of the Christian Church is drawn in the New Testament, not from the institutions made by man. The Christian Church does not arise from human culture but descends into human culture to redeem it from within.

THE KEY

The gospel and church growth are vitally connected. Neither can function without the other. The gospel must interpenetrate everything that church growth is and does, and church growth must be as vitally connected and responsive to the gospel as a physical arm is to a living person.

Church growth is a concept that is at home in the very Body of Christ among men, *here and now.* Growth is life-unfolding. It certainly means enlargement in a measurable way, but the analogy of enlargement as a mere addition of arms and legs is not quite right. Growth has more to do with maturation, changes which are necessary in order to relate to the enlarging demands and opportunities of life. Church growth in the gospel sense is the power of God unto salvation, transforming individuals and the society in which they live. Primarily, the gospel dynamic is redemption that unlocks the potential of every person. God's grace sets us free to be what God made us to be.

The gospel is the key to the task of the growing Church. The gospel of Jesus Christ turns the world upside down and sets norms of success straight that have been distorted by self-interest. The Church is God's life among men, fitted to man's needs, but everlastingly clashing with the structures of human selfishness.

The Church Was Jesus' Concern

Paul declares, "Our great God and Savior, Jesus Christ . . . gave himself for us to redeem us from all wickedness and to purify for himself a people that are his very own, eager to do what is good" (Titus 2:13-14).

The apostle Paul, in particular, grasped the enormous truth that the purpose of Jesus' coming was to establish in the world a body of people which would become His own extended self, to be a witness to Him by a dynamic interpenetration into every nook and cranny of the world of people.

The interesting and important fact about the Chris-

tian life is that neither Jesus nor Paul left it in a fog of
abstraction nor in the sentimentality of human shallow-
ness.

No Christian exists outside the Body of Christ. The
definition of being Christian is to be "in Christ," and the
entrance into His Body is His to determine. The conditions
are His, the agenda for Christian life development and
service is His, not ours.

JESUS' MANDATE FOR THE CHURCH

It is the Church, or Christ's Body, that is to grow.
Whatever it means for the Church to be called into service
by God, to take up the ministry of Christ, is what church
growth must mean.

One of the most powerful and compelling events in
Jesus' life with His disciples occurred in the darkest hour
of the disciples' experience. Their shattered faith after
Jesus' death caused them to be huddled together, locked in
against those who had killed their supposed Messiah (see
Luke 24:21), lest they too be arrested and killed.

Jesus appeared to them with the startling words, "As
the Father has sent me, *I am sending you.*" Then the significant act: Jesus breathed into them *His* breath and
said, "Receive the Holy Spirit" (the expected "sign" of the
Messiah).

Before the disciples could recover their poise on hearing this, Jesus continued, "If you forgive anyone his sins,
they are forgiven; if you do not forgive them, they are not
forgiven" (John 20:21-23). Here is the divine clue to the
meaning of church growth.

In these words lie the meaning and authority and
power of the Church. God intends the Church to be the
agent through which the world finds forgiveness and not

condemnation, even as Christ himself came not to condemn but to save.

The Community of Love

In this amazing, brief event lies the basic core of the *meaning* of the Church, the *power* of the Church, and the *mandate* for it. The Church is not self-created but almost literally picked up off the floor and put together out of the broken scraps of humanity and made over "in Christ" the Lord. "In Christ," lost individuals can "find out who they are" in the Christian community, to be true persons within the True Person. The mandate for the Church of God, over which Christ is Lord, is to create in the world a community of love, in which the world can experience the love of Christ.

The following is a brief statement of the introduction of the respective principles of church growth in the gospel sense.

Gospel Principles of Church Growth

The Church Is God's Creation

Christian converts are "in Christ" by grace. The Church is an *organism* (the extension of Christ's life) before it is an organization. It is not merely an aggregate of believing individuals who are in fellowship or congenial social units in which human tensions are in some measure resolved.

Christ Is the Head of the Church

The Church *confronts* the world. It does not reflect the sinful prejudices of the world. It should be an incarnation of Christlikeness *(agape)* much as Christ was God incarnate. It is in the world as comfortably as Jesus was (eating with sinners)—but no more comfortable than He was (the world killed Him).

Love, Christ's New Commandment

Entrance into the Church is determined by its Head. Christ is Lord. His Word prevails. By "accepting Christ," we accept His Lordship in which His Saviorhood resides (2 Pet. 1:11). The "royal law . . . 'Love your neighbor as yourself'" (Jas. 2:8) is not an option but a command. "A new commandment I give you: Love one another. As I have loved you, so you must love one another" (John 13:34).

EPHESIANS—A MODEL FOR THE CHURCH

Resting, one must presume, in a Roman prison, Paul had time to distill the essence of all he had taught about the Christian faith and its meaning in practical Christian life. In his Epistle entitled Ephesians, that essence is recorded. The theme of Christ is that essence and brings into form the glorious "edifice" of the Church as His Body in the world.

Every Pauline theological strand begins here and extends outward to its practical involvement.

Ephesians is a sort of code to the whole of the gospel as interpreted by Paul. Standing in sharp outline are these teachings about the Church—the essence of the gospel. The Church is God's creation. Before creation, mankind was intended to be "in Christ," holy and blameless, and to reveal God's praise. *In Christ* all things are to be united. All alienations are ended in Him: "He is our peace . . . [having] broken down the dividing wall of hostility" (Eph. 2:14, RSV). *In Christ,* the Church was created for good works "which God prepared beforehand, that we should walk in them" (v. 10, RSV). Christ is the Chief Corner-stone "in whom the whole structure is joined together and grows into a holy temple . . . you also are built into it," he said, "for a dwelling place of God in the Spirit" (vv. 21-22, RSV). *In Christ,* all are fellow citizens and members of the household of God.

For the purpose of this growth toward unity in Christ, the services of the members are called (1) to equip the saints for the work of the ministry, (2) for building up the Body of Christ, (3) "speaking the truth in love, . . . to grow up in every way into him who is the head, into Christ, from whom the whole body, joined and knit together by every joint with which it is supplied, when each part is working properly," (4) "makes bodily growth and upbuilds itself in love" (Eph. 4:15-16, RSV).

THE CHURCH IS PEOPLE

The most amazing thing about Paul's magnificent concept of the Church is the fact that God uses us as specific individuals in it. No part of the Church as the Body of Christ is mere excess baggage. No one can expect to go along for the ride. Membership is not, for Paul, a name on a roll book, but an organ or vital extension to a living body, seen or unseen, but essential to the health and usefulness of the whole body. The eye or hand is obviously important, but equally so is the liver or some minute, deeply hidden gland. The whole body suffers when any part decides to lie down on the job.

The importance of the individual cannot be overemphasized. In Christian community, the true meaning of person emerges. Personal worth and personal moral stature are born in the atmosphere of God's acceptance of us and in the interaction of God-accepted persons in Christian community.

When by grace God calls us *by our name* (not, "Hey, you, come here"), a major reconstruction of how one thinks of himself begins to take place. Those who are beaten almost to death by the injustices of society find that a great Someone is "the lifter up of [one's] head" (Ps. 3:3, KJV). True individualism is created when the person begins to realize that God has entrusted each one with a purpose and mission—to be an interpreter of the gospel.

GOD USES US AS HIS INTERPRETERS

It is one thing to grasp the larger meaning of *Church;* it is quite another to be confronted with the fact that each individual is a living "cell" in it, a cell essential to the health of the whole.

Human nature has received a "bad press" in much theology. It has often seemed more "religious" to depreciate the humanity of mankind and thereby subtly to excuse it from becoming what God's grace is given to make of it.

God uses us! This unbelievable fact underlies every assertion that God loves us and that He expects certain responses from us that would be impossible without His love.

THE HOLY SPIRIT AND HUMAN NATURE

Church growth requires people. People cannot produce church growth without the Holy Spirit. Such a statement raises the fundamental question: Why does the Holy Spirit work through people? The answer to this question will throw light on the meaning of spiritual gifts.

Are spiritual gifts natural or supernatural? The answer to this question lies squarely on theological presuppositions. If one's theology cannot find a way to accept the spiritual acceptability of "natural man," then the work and ministry of the Holy Spirit must bypass the natural talents and abilities of man. Gifts, then, must be non-natural additions to the human person, literal "endowments" which have no roots in the person.

The problem is how we are to regard nature, or the natural person. Are nature and grace set against each other, or is there a vital "at-home-ness" in their interaction?

Something of a solution could be useful were we to remember that the *natural* is also God's creation. All gifts are God-given. No one has gifts he has not received. Man was made to be indwelt by the Spirit. Man is not less human as a sinner than he is as a Christian.

Made in God's Image

Christ is God's Image. The most significant thing that can be said about man is that with all his humanness, his limitations and fallibility, with all his ignorance and finiteness, he is made in God's image. In our nature as human persons there is reflected something so essential to God's nature that it raises man to a height and grandeur that can never be lost so long as he is man.

Man may degrade himself, debauch himself, ruin his powers, but he cannot "unhumanize" himself. This is both his glory and his shame.

What is it about God that informs us about ourselves? The answer is Christ. We can only understand ourselves as we look at Christ. Our finite bodies mark us off from other selves, even from God's self. We are individuals and capable of intelligent and meaningful decision only because we are also bodies.

It is precisely the body which allows for any human intelligence, moral life, or religion to be possible. This body is essential to us. It is not a prison to our spirits nor an enemy to be defeated and discarded, but it is rather the vessel which contains all our powers, the communication center of personality.

Wesleyan theology begins with a concept of God in Christ. Christ reveals God and man in himself. Christ came to save us from sin—"if not sin here and now, from what does Christ save us?" asked Wesley.

The Enabling Grace

A careful biblical study of the terms used for those avenues of grace by means of which the Holy Spirit is poured out into the Church and from the Church into the world will reveal an important truth. The word for "divine gift" speaks of a real but intangible quality of love which does not become a possession but a relationship out of which love flows so long as that relationship with the Source is sustained.

A better analogy than a bestowal of some possession which one can claim as his own, and more true to the intent of the biblical writers, is to understand the relationship of the Holy Spirit to us as an enabling grace, a vitalizing of the whole person. The dynamic of the Holy Spirit awakens dormant abilities in us, utilizes what we have "presented to God" to the purposes of His will. Those drab capacities which we often downgrade as useless, or those splashy abilities we misused which are now "presented to God" as a vital part of our "whole body," are now available to God, "set on fire" as it were, to achieve far more than ever could be achieved by ourselves.

It is the whole person that God needs, not a mere premise upon which to act. Gifts cannot be properly considered as a sprinkling of unrelated gems distributed here and there. Charismata is the activity of the Holy Spirit in the Church, pouring grace and love into the lives of those who need God by means of persons who are open enough to Him to cooperate fully.

The Gift to the Church

The Holy Spirit is the abiding presence of God in His shrine (1 Cor. 3:16)—the Church. Each individual is an integral part of that shrine and participates in the life of the Spirit. God's Spirit belongs in that community, not as a visitor but as the very life of it. Every individual has, in a real sense, contributed himself to that community, not to lose his identity but precisely to find it, where alone one's true self can be authentic and maturing. In that community the Holy Spirit operates in the world.

Importance of the Laity

The contemporary interest in spiritual gifts is evidence of the growing understanding of the importance of the laity. For too long, a radical dualism between clergy and lay people has tended to discourage vital lay participation in the church.

Each individual in the Church is important. No concept of the importance of the individual in all of human thought holds the creative tension between the social nature of man and his personal integrity so wholesomely as does the Christian faith. God is not the Victim of His own nature, but the Author of the freedoms He maintains for His created beings.

The call to present the body a living sacrifice to God is an eloquent commentary to the oneness of personality which the biblical writers always taught. We are not three selves (body, soul, spirit) but a single self. The trichotomy idea of the human state is a Greek, not a Hebrew idea, and lies at the foundation of most heretical teachings that

60

have arisen about Christ and His Church. It is precisely the unified self presented whole and holy (Rom. 12:1) to God for His service that is required. "O God," sang Charles Wesley, "Thine own I am. Now, I give back Thine Own." It is that whole self that God needs in His service, not as a clod on which or in which He does His work in the world, but *with whom* He works and whom He trusts with the high calling in Jesus. An integrated self, the goal of sanctification, is the self God needs.

FRUIT OF THE SPIRIT IN 1 CORINTHIANS 13

The Love Chapter, 1 Corinthians 13, is not a misplaced sentimental "poem" but the very core of Paul's theology of gifts.

The priority of love over gifts is a Pauline theme. In Galatians he speaks of the importance of love as fulfilling the whole law which is expressed in one word, "Love your neighbor as yourself" (Gal. 5:14). This was Jesus' teaching, quoted from the Old Testament, a truth linking the Christian gospel with all of revelation. But Paul sees this basic truth as the evidence of the ministry of the Holy Spirit. "The fruit of the Spirit is love . . ." The gifts are verified by love which is the fruit of the Spirit. Any of the gifts can be faked or misused (1 Cor. 13:1-3), but fruit cannot be.

First Corinthians 13 provides the perspective by which to evaluate gifts and describes the function that gifts are designed to serve when they are bearers of evangelical love.

THE FRUIT OF THE SPIRIT AND SPIRITUAL GIFTS

The gifts of the Spirit cannot be divorced from the fruit of the Spirit which is love. Gifts and love belong together in the same package. Gifts are nothing but noise ("a clanging cymbal") without love, and love is only genuine when it is an expression of the desire to build up the Body of Christ. Gifts and fruit (love) must be two sides of one's personal relationship to God and one's fellows.

The amazing truth is emerging that gifts and fruit are really not from different sources at all but are two sides of one thing. Gifts are none other than the expression of the Spirit, just as His fruit is. Frank Carver, in an unpublished paper, quotes Michael Green, with appreciation, from *I Believe in the Holy Spirit*.

> The charismatic gifts are nothing other than the gifts of God's love. They begin with our redemption. They include the heightening of qualities already present or latent within us, such as gifts of administration, leadership, teaching, marriage, celibacy. These natural qualities can be *charismatic* if, and so long as, they are dedicated to the service of the Lord and the building up of the people in the strength that He gives. If they are used selfishly they can be disastrous.

Carver's own position is expressed in these words:

> Significant for our approach as Wesleyans to the spiritual gifts is that they are not arbitrarily "added" to the lives of certain otherwise quite ordinary believers. Rather they consist of and flow out of all that a Christian is as essentially constituted by the grace of God brought to bear by God in His sovereign freedom on the concrete and unique situations and tasks of every Christian.

In other words, one who has presented all his God-given human "equipment" to God as his gift, is the vehicle through whom the grace of God, by the Holy Spirit, can be manifested to the world.

SPIRITUAL GIFTS ARE FOR RECONCILIATION

The effect of all this is—or should be—that an atmosphere of love and acceptance and healing is thrown around those who are imprisoned in sin and are too help-less to break out of it. Before these imprisoned people even begin to ask for help (or are perhaps too proud to ask, or may be unaware that they need help, or that help is available), the Church should be on the alert and ready to help in a way that will speak to them. If we are doing Jesus' work, we will build bridges of love and acceptance over which the meeting of lives can take place. As forgiveness was available before ever we could do anything about a meeting with Christ, so we need to initiate that meeting with others. Reconciliation is the kind of forgiveness that is our job description.

All the gifts center around this one grand purpose—to be reconcilers. In fact, love/forgiveness/reconciliation is the meaning of gifts. All these gifts have this one thing in common—to demonstrate in actual life the message and living reality of Jesus' love for people.

In the interest of the Church as Christ's Body in the world, we must understand ourselves as the forgiving, reconciling, redemptive community called to this by the Lord himself. In this context, gifts of the Spirit have meaning.

WESLEYAN CONCEPTS OF GIFTS

In the light of the foregoing background study, the following understanding of spiritual gifts emerges.

1. The term "gifts" as used in church growth is asso-ciated with the idea of the *Church in action*. However "gifts" are defined, the reaching out, sharing, communica-tion aspect is implied. Religious experience has turned outward toward others.

2. "Spiritual gifts" emphasizes the *importance of individuals* to the whole ministry of the Church, as over against the traditional and sometimes artificial distinc-

tions between clergy and lay people that excuses the lay person from such responsibility and often forbids it.

3. Being the recipient of "gifts" can lead to a more *wholesome concept of the community* dimension of the Church.

4. As a responsible member (part of the Body), the full potential of everyone is enhanced. Everyone is important, not as a mere statistic to be counted, but as a *resource person* contributing essential life and value to the Body. We are not merely consumers but producers. *"God uses us."* Nothing taught in Scripture permits us to justify any one-way submissionism to humiliate, repress, or inhibit the leadership capacities or any talents of another, or to arbitrarily take the authority of deciding for others which spiritual gifts others are permitted to exercise.

5. In the realm of gifting it must be kept in mind that we as human persons are made by God. Whatever capacities we have were intended on God's part to make the kind of creature He could commune with.

The Holy Spirit is at home in the kind of person God made. Every aspect of human nature makes the abiding Holy Spirit at home. We were never intended to be without that intimate relationship of the Spirit. True natural man *is* the host of the Holy Spirit. Mankind was made to be the medium of God's Spirit in His ministry in the world. Sin is the closing off of that medium from the inside. It is ourselves rejecting the purpose of our creation, robbing God of His creature, "dead to God," and attempting to use the enormous capacities of our created potential to serve ourselves. This is the ultimate robbery, the ultimate defiance, the ultimate desecration.

6. "Natural talents," redeemed by the blood of Christ, are what God is asking from us. *He made* us and He is asking us to return what He entrusted to us.

1. In what way is the gospel essential to church growth?

2. What is the Church? What does growth mean in relation to the Church?

3. Discuss the implication of the Church as God's creation. How does anyone enter God's Church? Who can be members?

4. Jesus Christ united in himself (in His very body) all the divisions of mankind, all the antagonism, all the hatreds. What does this mean practically?

5. Jesus was God's Interpreter. What does this mean?

6. In what way are we to be interpreters? Would substituting "witnesses" for "interpreters" make any difference in what this means to you? Explain.

7. In what way are spiritual gifts natural? Supernatural? What do you mean by "natural" and "supernatural"?

8. Why do we call the gifts "spiritual"?

9. Discuss the relationship of fruit and gifts.

10. Fruit is personal and gifts are community related. How? Why?

4

ROMANS, 1 CORINTHIANS: Spiritual Job Descriptions

By Morris Weigelt

The whole redemptive process is a lavish gift of God to sinful man. In response to the obedience of man, God gives His Holy Spirit to enhance, enrich, and stabilize the believer for Kingdom purposes.

The Old Testament presents a wide variety of metaphors which expect the completion of the purposes of God among His people. Primary among these passages are the references to the day when unity and wholeness and perfection shall be visible. Then the age of the Messiah will indeed have come.

The writers of the New Testament understand that these marvelous promises have been fulfilled in the coming of Christ. The Messiah has indeed come. Jesus' own understanding is reflected in His inaugural message at Nazareth when He read the passage from Isaiah 61. This passage emphasizes the release of the captive, the restoration of sight to the blind, the freeing of the downtrodden, and the proclamation of the Jubilee celebration; and the proclamation of the gospel to the poor. Jesus' comment on the passage must have been electrifying: "Today this Scripture has been fullfilled in your hearing" (Luke 4:21, NASB).

The Day of Pentecost was recognized as the climax of the Messianic promises by those who participated. What God had promised in Joel was now a visible reality, and the unity of the community of believers was powerfully noted again and again in the Book of Acts.

The net result of this new, and long-awaited, flow of the Holy Spirit was transformation through reconciliation. Introversion and selfishness were no longer the norm. Paul well expressed the reorientation: "For the love of Christ controls us, having concluded this, that one died for all, therefore all died; and He died for all, that they who live should no longer live for themselves, but for Him who died and rose again on their behalf" (2 Cor. 5:14-15, NASB). Paul never tired of declaring that life was no longer to be wasted on personal desires, but to be spent for Kingdom purposes.

THE NEW PRIORITY

The new priority was the priority of the Body of Christ —the community of believers. The "God of all comfort . . . comforts us in all our affliction . . . with the comfort with which we ourselves are comforted by God" (2 Cor. 1:3-4, NASB). God does not lavish His grace upon us for our own good alone, but that the whole Body may benefit. It is in this vein of thought that Paul urged the Corinthians: "Seek to abound for the edification of the church" (1 Cor. 14:12, NASB).

In the Ephesian discussion of the distribution of the gifts of Christ (note the easy alternation between God and Christ and the Holy Spirit in the discussion of the gifts),

Paul first notes that the primary goal is the completion of the unity of the Body. Note how he changes the plural subject into a singular object-goal: "Until we all attain to the unity of the faith, and of the knowledge of the Son of God, to a mature man, to the measure of the stature which belongs to the fulness of Christ" (Eph. 4:13, NASB). The same sequence and goal appear in verses 15 and 16: "We are to grow up in all aspects into Him, who is the head, even Christ, from whom the whole body, being fitted and held together by that which every joint supplies, according to the proper working of each individual part, causes the growth of the body for the building up of itself in love" (NASB).

There is no question in these discussions of the gifts of the Spirit but that the primary responsibility of the recipients of those gifts is contribution to the Body. The gifts are distributed so that the reconciled individuals may contribute to the growth of the Body. *The highest priority is the Body.*

THE PROPER ATTITUDE

The 12th chapter of Romans provides a powerful description of the attitude of the individual member of the Body of Christ. In the previous chapter Paul has been discussing the role of physical Israel in the purposes of God. In Rom. 11:29 he refers to the privileges of election for Israel and says, "For the gifts and the calling of God are irrevocable" (NASB).

The 12th chapter begins with a call to sanctification. There is no room for halfhearted service. The demands of God are total and His response is reconciliation, transformation, and renewal. The grace of God now flows through the obedient believer.

Paul is quick to note in the third verse that the gift of

God's grace is no cause for undue pride. He calls for each Christian to have an accurate assessment of himself by each member of the community in the presence of, and under the grace of, God. Paul uses his apostolic authority to ask each member "not to think more highly of himself than he ought to think; but to think so as to have sound judgment, as God has allotted to each a measure of faith" (NASB).

The problem of exaggerated self-esteem is quickly solved by the recognition that God in His sovereignty has distributed to each man according to His decision. The object and verb in this significant sentence come from the same root and might be translated: "God has measured a determined measure [or allotted a fixed allotment] to each person." The rhetorical question then is: If God has provided these abilities and functions, who can use these capacities for a matter of pride?

The "measure of faith" here is obviously not saving faith, for salvation is not a matter of degrees or proportion.

In verses 4 and 5 Paul turns to that favorite metaphor of the body as an analogy to teach us the proper attitude of the individual within the Body of Christ. There are many members with a variety of functions. These diverse functions are all necessary and together "we, who are many, are one body in Christ, and individually members one of another" (NASB). Mutual interdependence requires that we have the proper attitude toward each other and toward the whole.

In verses 6 through 8 Paul gives us some of his notorious incomplete sentences—the main verb is absent. The verbal idea in verse 6 is evidently dependent upon the main verb in verse 5 and could be translated: "We, who are many, are one body . . . while possessing differing gifts according to the grace given to us." The flow of God's grace through the obedient believer is a gift which is to be exercised (the NASB supplies this verb to make clearer the sense of verse 6) in light of that grace.

THE DIFFERENT GIFTS WITHIN THE BODY (ROMANS 12)

Seven different gifts (note that the word "gift" is used in a more limited meaning now than in 11:29) are listed in connection with the qualification which controls the operation of the particular gift. The implication is that each gift is to be exercised without undue self-esteem or undue self-effacement within the diversity and mutual interdependence of the Body. Only under such a procedure will the Body of Christ operate as God has designed it to operate.

Prophecy

The first gift listed is that of "prophecy." The concept of prophet already has a long history prior to the New Testament usage. Jesus was identified in the Gospels as a prophet with reference to His miraculous powers (Luke 13:33-34) and His teaching ability with authority and wisdom (Luke 4:21-24; 7:39; Mark 1:22; 6:2 ff.). The task of the prophet is the proclamation of the great revelation of God through the power of the Holy Spirit. The New Testament references indicate that the gift of prophecy was operative both in individual settings and in group settings. In 1 Corinthians prophecy is granted a high rank in the catalog of gifts because it contributes directly to the upbuilding of the Church.

The prophet is to exercise this gift of inspired proclamation and teaching "according to the proportion of his faith" (NASB). The meaning of this phrase is probably that the prophet is to disclose his message in conformity ("proportion" is a word used in mathematics and is found nowhere else in the New Testament) to the whole revelation of God.

The prophet is subject to the community as well, and his contribution is to be tested by the community (1 Cor. 14:29; 1 Thess. 5:19ff.; 1 John 4:1). Even the prophet stands within the community as one among many members in the one Body.

Serving

The second gift in the Romans list is "ministry" or "serving." The Greek word here is the common one used in the New Testament for general Christian ministries with special attention to charity and bodily needs. It is the origin of our English word "deacon," although it probably has a more general meaning in the New Testament—note the choice of deacons in Acts 6 (but also note that the apostles were going to devote themselves to the *ministry* —same word—of the Word). It is unusual to find the word for ministry in this particular list of the gifts of the Spirit sandwiched in between prophecy and teaching.

The qualification for this gift is that it be exercised in the same way that the gift of prophecy is exercised—in accordance with the proportion of faith. The person through whom the Holy Spirit flows in service is to be content to serve without wishing to either prophesy or teach. The gift of ministry is just as important to the proper functioning of the Body.

Teaching

The third gift is "teaching." The Greek word here technically refers to the person who is doing the teaching, rather than to the gift of teaching in and of itself. Again Jesus was a beautiful model of this function. He was known for His teaching ability which swept aside the endless debates of the rabbis of contemporary Judaism and went to the heart of the issue (for example, the way in which the Sermon on the Mount handles the delicate matters of the details of the Law). The gift of teaching is the ability to share the basic truths of the kingdom of God with clarity and insight and to aid the hearer to see the interrelationships and implications of the new material.

The teacher is urged to allow the grace of the Holy Spirit to flow through him in explaining and outlining the basic truths of the Kingdom to others for the good of the whole Body of Christ. The teacher is to exercise the gift of teaching without undue pride, or undue humility, as a responsible member of the Body.

Encouragement

The fourth gift is that of "exhortation" or "encouragement." Again the emphasis is on the person doing the exhortation and not on the gift itself. The one who exhorts is particularly skilled in encouraging, comforting, and strengthening through inspiration. The Greek word is a form of the word Paraclete—the designation of the Holy Spirit in the Gospel of John and the designation of Jesus in the First Epistle of John. Again Jesus is a model of this gift which is to be exercised for the common good without undue boasting or self-effacement.

Giving, Leadership, Mercy

The last three gifts give attention to the attitude in which the gift is used. In each case the primary emphasis is upon the person through whom God is working: "he who gives"; "he who leads"; and "he who shows mercy" (NASB). The qualifier in each case is clearly attitudinal. The person with the gift of giving is urged to exercise that gift, according to the grace given to him, with liberality.

The Greek word for liberality emphasizes both generosity and simplicity or frankness. The one who leads must do so according to the flow of God's grace through him. The qualifier makes reference to earnest diligence which strives to complete the task as quickly as possible.

The final gift in the list enables the person motivated and moved by God's Spirit to extend aid to those who are in trouble—the poor, the sick, the stranger. The Greek word here is used in the New Testament both for the giving of aid and the giving of money (alms). The primary attitude here is one of gladness and graciousness.

The primary theme of the whole chapter is repeated in verse 16: "Be of the same mind toward one another; do not be haughty in mind, but associate with the lowly. Do not be wise in your own estimation" (NASB). The framework for the section is highlighted when we remember that the opening two verses of the chapter are: "I urge you therefore, brethren, by the mercies of God, to present your bodies a living and holy sacrifice, acceptable to God, which is your spiritual service of worship. And do not be conformed to this world, but be transformed by the renewing of your mind, that you may prove what the will of God is, that which is good and acceptable and perfect" (NASB).

The proper operation of the gifts of the Spirit within the Body of Christ is beautifully presented in this chapter. Emphasis lies on the attitude with which each member participates in the Body. God allots the gifts. The gifts are operative only through the grace of God flowing through the fully consecrated and sanctified members of the Body of believers. And the crowning attitude is that of love as it is modeled in Christ.

Note once again that the primary thrust of these gifts is toward the life of the Body itself.

In the Romans 12 discussion of spiritual gifts, emphasis rests on the proper attitude of the individual who exercises the gift by the grace of God. In the 1 Corinthians 12 discussion of spiritual gifts the primary emphasis rests on the Source of the gifts as the God who distributes and guides the use of the gifts for the upbuilding of the whole Body.

The opening verses of 1 Corinthians 12 clearly indicate that the gifts are distributed for the purpose of confessing Jesus as Lord. The setting implies that some excesses at Corinth were clearly not the work of the Holy Spirit and were therefore not spiritual gifts. All spiritual gifts contribute to the glorification of Jesus as Lord and not to the glorification of the individual.

The keynote of the passage is struck in verses 4-6. Note the parallelism in structure:

4: Apportionments of gifts—the same Spirit
5: Apportionments of ministries—the same Lord
6: Apportionments of effects—the same God

The parallelism emphasizes the basic unity of the gifts as distributions of God. It also emphasizes the sovereign distribution of the one God who apportions gifts according to His design.

"Apportionments" is translated by the King James Version as "diversities"; by the *New International Version* as "different kinds"; and by the *Revised Standard Version* and the *New American Standard Bible* as "varieties." The Greek word can mean either "difference," "distinction," "distribution," "apportionment," "allotment," or "variety." The meaning in this paragraph is shown by the reappearance of the word as a verb in verse 11: "But one and the same Spirit works all these things, *distributing* to each one individually just as He wills" (NASB). The emphasis does not lie in the fine distinctions between the different gifts, but in the allotment and apportioning of the gifts throughout the Body for the common good by God himself.

The very same Spirit who enables the believers to confess Jesus as Lord operates in and through the gifts for the edification of the Body of Christ—the Church. "But to each one is given the manifestation of the Spirit for the common good" (1 Cor. 12:7, NASB). "The manifestation of the Spirit" may be understood either as that which reveals or displays the Spirit, or the result which the Spirit produces. Recall that the primary manifestation of the Spirit is the confession of the Lordship of Jesus (v. 3).

The emphasis here upon "common good" refers to either advantage or profit. The sovereign distribution of the Holy Spirit provides gifts which flow through the believers for the advantage of the Body of Christ.

1 Cor. 12:8-12

Paul now turns to another of his lists of the spiritual gifts. There is an interesting variety in these lists, indicating they are suggestive rather than exhaustive lists.

Wisdom, Knowledge

Verse 8 makes a distinction between the communication of wisdom and the communication of knowledge. The precise meanings in the specific setting at Corinth may not be fully recoverable. The basic distinctions, however, are clear from the rest of the Corinthian correspondence. The Corinthians suffered from a false concept of wisdom, and Paul is careful to point out that true wisdom flows from God. Such wisdom is insight and comprehension of the deep things of God—especially the "mystery" of salvation. Wisdom evidently includes knowledge, but is characterized by spiritual comprehension and insight in application of knowledge in specific settings.

Wisdom is to be exercised "through the Spirit" and knowledge is to be used "according to the same Spirit" (NASB). Knowledge involves the use of reason and the communication of facts. Both wisdom and knowledge are a part of the essential function of teaching within the Body.

Faith, Healing, Miracles

Verse 9 introduces the gift of faith as a manifestation of the Spirit in the life of the believer. This is obviously not saving faith, but probably the faith which works wonders. The next two items in the list reinforce this understanding—"gifts of healing" and "the effecting of miracles" (NASB). The three are clearly related gifts. Orr and Walter speak of faith as the "kind of openness and confidence that enable the power of God to operate through the person who has it."[1] The miraculous operations of the Spirit for the advantage of the community operate through responsive believers.

Discernment

Since the work of the Spirit is subject to deceptive abuses, the gift of the Spirit called "discerning of spirits" (KJV) is the ability to identify the counterfeit. Such discrimination was absolutely essential to the future of the Church—especially in a setting like that of Corinth and places where Gnosticism was attempting to pollute the Body of Christ. Such discriminatory powers are a gift of the Spirit for the protection of the Church.

Pride Is out of Place

Since the Spirit is the Distributor, all pride is out of place. Paul had already touched this issue in 4:7: "For who regards you as superior? And what do you have that you did not receive? But if you did receive it, why do you boast as if you had not received it?" (NASB). How often the Church (and particularly individual members) have fallen into the trap of valuing the gift and failing to see the Giver!

Verse 12 summarizes the whole section effectively. The unity of the Body of Christ comes from the effective operation and manifestation of the Spirit. The diversity is not denied, but it is caught up in the higher concept of the priority of the Body. In the highest and richest sense, the fellowship of the Body of Christ is the most powerful unity available this side of the Second Coming.

1 COR. 12:27-28

The next section of 1 Corinthians 12 effectively uses the analogy of the body to show mutual dependence and interrelatedness of the individual members with the specific gifts distributed to them by the Spirit. All care for each other. All suffer when one suffers. All rejoice when one rejoices. There is no room for any kind of division.

The climax of this discussion is found in verse 27: "Now you are Christ's body, and individually members of it" (NASB). Paul then proceeds to yet another of the list of the gifts with a mixture of function and manifestation of the Spirit. Again the sovereign operation of God in the process is visible in the verb "appointed."

Apostle

The list begins with the gift of apostle (v. 28). New Testament usage reserves the term "apostle" for the select group of the Twelve. Paul includes himself in that category and a few others who were not members of the Twelve. Scholars are divided on the distinct connotation of the term in this passage. Some understand it to refer to the select group described above. Others see it as a specialized gift for the continuation of the church. (Note the comment on this gift in chapter five.)

Prophets, Teachers, Miracles, Helps

The next two gifts in the list are "prophets" and "teachers" which we have already defined. "Miracles" would correspond to the gift mentioned in verse 10 above. The "gifts of healings" (NASB) were also mentioned above. The next two items on the list are "helps" and "administrations" (NASB). "Helps" refers to helpful deeds which give aid or benefit or kindness to someone else. It is largely a one-to-one relationship which receives little notoriety.

Administrations

"Administrations" comes from a Greek word which refers to the sternsman or pilot of a ship. He controls the direction of the ship and coordinates the work of the other members of the crew. It is interesting that these two gifts which appear in the middle of the list are not repeated in verses 29 and 30.

Only a Few

Paul now turns to show that this list of gifts is not a combination given to every individual in the Body, but that only a few exercise the function indicated. The rhetorical questions repeated so frequently underscore once again the distribution which God chooses in the right proportion and mixture for the common good of the Church. "Not all are apostles, are they? Not all are prophets, are they? Not all are teachers, are they? Not all are workers of miracles, are they? Not all have gifts of healings, do they? Not all speak with tongues, do they? Not all interpret, do they?" (vv. 29-30, author's trans.). The obvious answer is: "No, they do not! Of course not! How foolish!"

The discussion of the differentiation of gifts within the Body is climaxed by the beautiful 13th chapter. Although not all the members of the community of faith have any one gift, all of them do have love—the more excellent way. Those who desire a special evidence of God's grace in their lives should seek for more love. Then the unity of the Spirit will be visible and the functioning of the Body will be enhanced and God's glory will be furthered. "Pursue love"! (1 Cor. 14:1, NASB).

DISCUSSION QUESTIONS

1. What is the biblical reason for the priority of the whole in the Body of Christ?

2. What is the proper attitude of the individual member of the Body toward himself?

3. According to Paul, how is each of the gifts listed in Rom. 12:6-8 to be exercised?

4. How does each of the gifts listed in Rom. 12:6-8 contribute to the whole Body?

5. Why do the majority of the gifts center on the needs of the Body itself?

6. Discuss the importance of the concept that God has apportioned the gifts according to His design.

7. What additional gifts are described in 1 Corinthians 12, and how do they contribute to the good of the whole?

FOR ADDITIONAL READING

Kinghorn, Kenneth Cain. *Gifts of the Spirit.* Nashville: Abingdon Press, 1976.

Purkiser, W. T. *The Gifts of the Spirit.* Kansas City: Beacon Hill Press of Kansas City, 1975.

Stedman, Ray C. *Body Life.* Glendale, Calif.: Regal Books, 1972.

5

PAUL'S THREE LETTERS:
Spiritual Gifts Are for Making Disciples

By Paul R. Orjala

In letters to three different young churches—to the Romans, to the Corinthians, and to the Ephesians—the apostle Paul indicated his deep concern for a healthy balance in the exercise of spiritual gifts. He was anxious that these churches not only focus their spiritual gifts toward ministries within the Body of Christ, but that they also develop outreach ministries that would help them fulfill their mission of making disciples.

SPIRITUAL GIFTS FUNCTION
BOTH INSIDE AND OUTSIDE THE CHURCH

There is probably only one gift that could be classified exclusively as an *outreach gift,* and that is the gift of the evangelist (Eph. 4:11). However, even that gift has a ministry inside the Body of Christ, in that it keeps the whole Body sensitized to the importance, the opportunities, and the means of evangelism.

On the other hand, evangelism is not the exclusive function of those who have the gift of the evangelist, but it is a function of the whole Body. At first glance, the rest of the gifts listed in these three classical passages on the spiritual gifts might appear to be classified simply as *maintenance gifts,* which they are primarily. As such, these maintenance gifts would be related to the outreach of the Body in at least three ways: (1) They minister to those involved in outreach and thus help make their outreach possible; (2) they prepare workers for involvement in outreach ministries (as through the teaching gift); and (3) they serve as adjunct ministries in discipling and caring for those who are brought into the Body through outreach evangelism.

However, on closer inspection of these maintenance gifts, we are led to the exciting discovery that all the gifts have a capacity for focusing directly on the outreach task of the Church in one way or another. In a very real sense, all Christians are called out of the world to become members of the Body of Christ in order to be sent back into the world as witnesses of the gospel.

ALL SPIRITUAL GIFTS MAY BE FOCUSED
ON THE EVANGELISTIC MINISTRY OF THE CHURCH

The principle of the unity of the Body requires that none of the gifts function in isolation from the others, not even the gift of the evangelist. Moreover, seldom is anyone won to Christ through the exclusive influence of one individual, but his conversion is usually the product of the ministry of many different people exercised in his behalf. Paul reminds the Corinthians, "I planted the seed, Apollos watered it, but God made it grow. So neither he who plants nor he who waters is anything, but only God, who makes things grow. The man who plants and the man who waters have one purpose, and each will be rewarded according to his own labor. For we are God's fellow workers; you are God's field, God's building" (1 Cor. 3:6-9).

The last section of this chapter will look in detail at how each of the gifts may be focused on the outreach ministry of the Church, but a quick inspection of each gift listed in the three chapters readily brings to mind instances in both the New Testament and in current church life where these gifts function dynamically for outreach. Even such gifts as leadership, administration, and giving may serve as facilitating ministries to make sure that evangelism can and does continue to happen through the action of the Body.

SPIRITUAL GIFTS SERVE THROUGH CHANNELS

Why is it, someone may ask, that music is not included in the lists of spiritual gifts? It is obviously used by God for ministry both inside and outside the Church. It seems to be a powerful tool for evangelism along with preaching, personal witness, the electronic media, and evangelistic writing.

It would seem that there are two reasons why music is not listed as a spiritual gift. First of all, its present form of use in worship and evangelism is a modern development which was unknown in New Testament times; though some forms of music were, of course, used in the times of both the Old Testament and the Early Church. More importantly, music is probably to be seen as a channel for exercising gifts rather than as a spiritual gift in and of itself. People may minister prophetically or evangelistically through music, especially through singing; and other gifts, such as encouraging as well, may be expressed through this channel.

As to whether there are more spiritual gifts, other

than those mentioned in the three New Testament passages, which can be focused in outreach evangelistic ministries—possibly some could be identified. No one of the three lists of gifts is comprehensive or complete, which should be a caution to us against stereotyping the definitions of spiritual gifts or list of them. On the other hand, probably some of the "gifts" we might want to add could be included under a flexible understanding of what some of the stated spiritual gifts could include as forms of ministry.

Spiritual Gifts Function for Both Service and Witness

Judging from the total range of spiritual gifts in the New Testament lists, we must conclude that God intends that the Body's outreach ministries include both evangelism and social concern (including social action at appropriate times). Witness and service are not competing but complementary ministries. Some liberals, in the guise of "ministering to the whole man," wind up ministering only to social and material needs, neglecting man's greatest need of salvation.

On the other hand, some ultrafundamentalist Christians allow themselves to be scared off by the spectre of the "social gospel" and wind up in the opposite corner where their sense of responsibility extends little beyond trying to get people into the kingdom of God. In this generation we are beginning to get back to a balanced both/and philosophy, like our spiritual predecessors in the early holiness movement in the 19th century.

The Cultural Mandate

One way of expressing both sides of the Christian responsibility is to speak of the *cultural mandate* and the *evangelistic (missionary) mandate.* The cultural mandate is related to the Christian life-style, and it speaks of how God expects us to live in fulfilling our *social responsibility* to our fellow human beings. The roots of the cultural mandate go back to the Old Testament where God gave man the responsibility of subduing the earth and all its creatures (Gen. 1:28) and after the Flood expanded the mandate to be understood as including also his stewardship of the lives of the other members of the human race (Gen. 9:1-7).

Jesus added His endorsement of this concept by linking to the Great Commandment ("love the Lord your God . . .") a second commandment to "Love your neighbor as yourself" (Matt. 22:36-39, quoting from Deut. 6:5 and Lev. 19:18). Jesus further identified what this love of neighbor was in the story of the Good Samaritan (Luke 10:30-37) and in the "inasmuch" passage (Matt. 25:31-46), where real believers are described as ministering to the hungry, the thirsty, the stranger, the naked, the sick, and those in prison. To make sure that the Body of Christ gets engaged in meeting such needs, God has given specialized outreach gifts in these areas not only to perform these ministries but also to keep us all reminded of our involvement as part of our Christian life-style.

THE EVANGELIST

The evangelistic (or missionary) mandate is stated in the Great Commission in its various forms in the Gospels and Acts. In its simplest form it may be stated as the mandate to "make disciples" (Matt. 28:19). This is the *essence* of the mission of the Church. Implicit in this command is also the mandate to plant churches, for baptizing and teaching are functions of the Church. Those with the gift of the evangelist give leadership in the Church in the task "to seek and to save" those that are lost (Luke 19:10). The gift of the apostle, as we shall see later, may be interpreted in part as involved in the implied task of church planting.

How can we maintain the proper biblical balance? First of all, by recognizing that the Holy Spirit is the One who gives the gifts "to each man, just as he determines" (1 Cor. 12:11). If He gives to *some* various gifts to be realized in service ministries, this is how *they* are to function in and for the Body. If He gives to *others* certain gifts to be realized in evangelistic ministries, this is the primary area of *their* responsibility for the Body.

On the other hand, we must not allow the doctrine of spiritual gifts to turn into a cop-out that releases us from responsibility in some of the areas in which we obviously are not gifted like others. We have already stated that the Christian life-style (as described in dozens of passages) requires us all to be responsive in fulfilling the cultural mandate, even though the gifts of some enable them to minister to physical and social needs far beyond our capacity and with greater effectiveness.

The same is true of the evangelistic mandate—we are all called to be witnesses (Acts 1:8) as part of our Christian life-style, even though some who are gifted for evangelism see far greater results than we do. Peter Wagner has described this relationship helpfully as the difference between the *gift* (which helps define the focus of ministry for individuals in the Body) and *role* (which identifies the various components of the Christian life-style in which we are all involved).

SPIRITUAL GIFTS AND ROLES
DEFINE THE SPHERE OF MINISTRIES

Where do each of us fit in all this? We can summarize it all up in terms of three levels of ministries which function inside and outside the Body of Christ.

1. *Role Ministries*

These role ministries are the same for all Christians. They could also be called **life-style ministries** because they are part of what it means to be a Christian. A Christian cares, helps, gives, encourages, serves, has compassion, witnesses. All Christians must cultivate these ministries. These are to be directed both inside and outside the Body of Christ.

2. *Body Life Ministries*

The body life ministries (Romans 12 and 1 Corinthians 12) are unique to each Christian as the Holy Spirit develops these special spiritual gifts in us. Not all Christians have these gifts, so we must exercise our particular gifts for the benefit of the Body of believers and the ministry of the Body in the world. Some of these gifts are especially suited for the outreach of the Church, but all of them may be focused in one way or another on the outreach ministries of the Church.

3. *Leadership Ministries*

Leadership ministries (Eph. 4:11) not only function directly inside and outside the Church but also help guide the Church, give it vision, and train the Church so that no essential ministries will be lacking. These are the apostle, the prophet, the evangelist, the pastor, and the teacher. They function for a twofold purpose: (1) to equip the saints for the work of ministry, and (2) to build up the Body of Christ (Eph. 4:12). These leadership ministries almost inevitably involve people with clusters of spiritual gifts. The purpose of leadership ministries is not to take ministry out of the hands of the laymen but to multiply ministry and to give it direction. Part of the direction that the ensemble of the five leadership ministries give to the Body of Christ is balance between maintenance and outreach.

These leadership gifts need to be exercised in the local church and also at the higher levels of church organization to help the church be the Church.

THE OUTREACH MINISTRIES OF THE BODY OF CHRIST

Let us now look at the individual gifts and how they may be focused on the outreach ministries of the Body in the world, keeping in mind that the service and witness ministries complement and aid each other in the fulfillment of the overall outreach goal of making disciples, which is the mission of the Church. For convenience, we shall treat the gifts in five groups according to their functions for the outreach of the Church.

1. *The facilitating gifts*

This first section includes leadership, administration, teaching, and giving. These gifts may focus on outreach by making it possible.

Leadership keeps an eye on goals and priorities to make sure that the Church does not just function as an end in itself. Leadership makes sure that the Church is working to fulfill both the cultural and the evangelistic mandates. It helps make plans in this direction, checks on results, and then modifies the plans if necessary to make sure that the Church does make disciples and ministers to people in need. Diligence marks the adequate functioning of this gift.

Administration works for the coordination and fulfilling of the outreach plans of the Church. When they bog down or go astray, it finds out what is wrong and helps to get things going again so the Church does not slip into a static state. It tries to see ahead and help provide for the future so that the necessary facilities and organization can be available to maximize the outreach opportunities of the Body.

Teaching keeps training programs going so that people's gifts may be adequately developed for full participation in the outreach ministries that they are appropriate for. It keeps information flowing so that people know what the current needs and opportunities are, so they can respond with the involvement of their gifts. Teaching may also be directly involved in training people to help themselves in some areas of physical and social needs, and may also be directly turned to evangelism (as in a Sunday school class) by helping people learn the content of the gospel and motivating people to move toward openness to receive Christ as their Savior. The test of true teaching is that people respond and learn.

Giving (or contributing) can obviously make many things possible by providing the necessary funds so that programs of outreach may be budgeted in proper balance with maintenance. The hallmark of giving as a spiritual gift is that it is done generously.

2. *The ministering gifts*

Serving, encouraging, mercy (or compassion), helping, and pastoral care comprise the ministering gifts. These gifts along with the sign gifts in the following section function in an area that might be called compassionate ministries. They are directed toward that area of outreach which is more directly related to the fulfilling of the social and physical needs included in the cultural mandate. They help confirm the gospel that we share and give a vivid example of the Christian life-style of self-giving love. They create readiness for people to respond to the claims of the gospel and give themselves to Jesus Christ.

The difference between the *serving* gift and the *helping* gift is usually considered to be that serving is more general and helping is more personal. Serving is an unusual ability to see needs and meet them, while helping is an unusual ability for making it possible or easier for other people to fulfill their tasks (and taking pleasure in doing this). These two gifts may open the door for witness or facilitate the ministry of the person with the gift of the evangelist, by taking care of such things as record keeping.

Mercy, or *compassion,* is to be exercised with cheerfulness so that it can be a witness to the quality of life that the gospel produces. It demonstrates the tenderness and sensitivity of Christian love and gives people a tantalizing taste of the koinonia fellowship that is found in the circle of love of the Church.

Pastoral care (Eph. 4:11) is one of the five leadership gifts, and the emphasis here is on the sense of responsibility that such a person has for keeping track of people and their needs, joys, and sorrows, and finding an appropriate way to respond to these needs. It is often a means whereby people are drawn to and drawn into the family of God. It is, by the way, not unique to pastors of churches; many laymen have been given the gift of a shepherd's heart.

3. *The sign gifts*

The gifts of faith, healing, miracles, and discernment of spirits are involved here. The first three gifts of this group are often called sign gifts because they are similar to Christ's miracles which are called "signs" in John's Gospel. The gift of discernment simply fits better here than with the other gifts.

In Matt. 11:2-6, when the disciples of John the Baptist were sent by John in prison to ask if Jesus were the expected Messiah, Jesus told them to return to John and report what they heard and saw: miracles of healing and resurrection and the preaching of the Good News to the poor. His miracles as demonstrations of the power of God were signs of who He was and of the Kingdom He was ushering in. In the Early Church, the miraculous powers demonstrated through the apostles served a similar purpose of authentication.

It is interesting that in the history of missions (and even today) when the gospel has been introduced among a new people for the first time, it is not uncommon for miracles of healing and other miracles to take place. The fact that this usually takes place among people with only an oral tradition (without a written language and hence without the Bible) is also interesting, for the miracles serve as an open communication and authentication that God is working through His people.

While we are justifiably cautious about claiming the appearance of these gifts and their effects in our day, we should not be surprised when God does choose to manifest himself through them. They do, however, seem to be subject to much misuse and misunderstanding. When the glory is attributed to God, they can have a strong effect for drawing people to the gospel, as well as relieving sickness and suffering and meeting other needs. These gifts are often considered to be not permanent gifts in many cases but given for specific healings or miracles, not to be repeated. There is not too much to be said about these gifts, for we do not know much about them except to recognize them when they are manifest.

The *discerning of spirits* is still unusual though perhaps a little more common, as it enables people to discriminate between what is genuine and what is counterfeit for the edification of the Body. It is a protection for God's people when someone is trying to deceive them. Positively it enables one to identify a true Christian with an almost uncanny certainty before any normal means of confirmation can take place. Such a gift is very helpful to the outreach ministries of the Body when it is given.

4. *The communication gifts*

Prophecy, wisdom, knowledge, languages, and interpretation of languages make up this vital area of communication gifts.

Prophecy or prophesying is the gift to proclaim God's message or interpret God's truth for a given occasion and for the individuals concerned. It can involve foretelling, but it most frequently involves forth-telling. It may be exercised in public or in private. It has the effect of making the hearers feel that God is speaking directly to them and to their situation. Preaching at its best has this element in it, but the gift may be exercised through other channels as well. Purkiser says, "God's part is to anoint; ours is to provide Him something to anoint by study, meditation, and prayer." Paul says, "If a man's gift is prophesying, let him use it in proportion to his faith" (Rom. 12:6).

Knowledge and *wisdom* as spiritual gifts are generally interpreted as contrasting in the way that insight and application differ. God gifts some people in the Church with unusual ability in conceptual thinking and other people with the ability to translate this into action and results. The Church certainly needs both kinds of people to apply their skills in outreach. We need "church growth thinkers" to guide and instruct us, but we especially need "church growth practitioners" to bring people into the Body of Christ as the Spirit uses them.

The gift of *languages* in Acts was obviously a cross-cultural and cross-linguistic gift of prophecy—God miraculously gave them the words to say to people who had a mother tongue that was different from their own. In 1 Corinthians 12—14, the language gift which is advocated is still a communication gift, since Paul rules out the use of tongues in ways that would block communication. There are differences of opinion in the details as to how this gift is to be understood today, but it cannot be denied that Paul condemns its misuse in the Corinthian church.

It is believed by many that a modern counterpart of the gift of languages may be found in the extraordinary ability that God gives to some missionaries to learn and utilize a new language for communicating the gospel with unusual results in evangelism and the upbuilding of the Church. It is an amazing fact that current linguistic research into glossolalia (tongues speaking) in both Christian and non-Christian religious groups reveals *no authenticated instance* in which the tongues speaking was identifiable as a natural language which the individual had not learned.

Interpretation of languages is likewise a gift which is explained in several different ways in our day. How it is understood depends on how the gift of languages is understood, but at the very least its biblical sense is that it serves to get God's message communicated to people who cannot understand the original utterance. Anyone who has lived or traveled where a foreign language is spoken realizes how vital this gift would be. God's message must be *understood* to be believed and acted upon. The interpretive gift, in both a narrow and extended sense, is vitally needed today as ethnic ministries loom large and both home and world mission opportunities increase. Both cultural and linguistic skills enhanced by the power of the Holy Spirit were never more needed.

5. *The church growth gifts*

The church growth gifts are but two: the gift of the evangelist and the gift of the apostle.

The gift of the evangelist is focused on the goal of the

Church's mission: making disciples (Matt. 28:19). Not every Christian has this gift (as in the case of the other gifts), but all Christians are to function as witnesses and develop their ability to lead others to Christ as the opportunity presents itself. The combination of this gift with others determines if the gift is to be exercised through preaching or in personal evangelism or both. It is both a lay and ministerial gift, for both public and private occasions. The proof of this gift is that people do in fact become Christians through the evangelist's efforts. There are thousands of Christians in whom this gift lies undeveloped because they have never learned how to exercise it. The recognition and deployment of this gift is one of the top priorities of the Church in our day.

The gift of the apostle is probably one of the least understood gifts of our day because Protestants have generally thought that its function ceased with the passing of the 12 apostles. However, the term is used in the New Testament to include other principal leaders in the Church such as James and also associates of Paul's in the missionary and church planting ministry. In fact, it was the technical name for the missionary in the Greek-speaking churches of the first two centuries.

The continuing significance of this gift today lies in the fact that it equips for the pioneer ministries on the frontiers of the church where it penetrates the world. It is the gift needed by general church leaders who must constantly push the church out into new areas geographically and functionally. It is the gift that equips for cross-cultural ministry in local churches, giving vision and means for outreach to other ethnic groups. It is the gift that creates the mind-set of the church planter who delights to go where there is nothing and with the help of the Spirit see the lost saved and become responsible members of the

Body of Christ. It is obviously the enduement that makes a missionary out of a missionary candidate.

And so we see that, although there are some gifts that function primarily for outreach, all the gifts may be focused for outreach in one way or another so that the Body of Christ may fulfill its mission of making disciples and building up the kingdom of God.

DISCUSSION QUESTIONS

1. In what sense is evangelism a "function of the whole Body"?

2. Why is music not included in the lists of spiritual gifts?

3. Explain the difference between the cultural mandate and the evangelistic (missionary) mandate.

4. What are life-style ministries

5. What are body life ministries?

6. What are leadership ministries?

7. What are the church growth gifts?

6

GOD'S WORD IN YOU:
How to Put Spiritual Gifts to Work

By Raymond W. Hurn

Now that we have a clearer biblical view of spiritual gifts, let us look at how each one of us fits into the Body of Christ.

Dr. C. Peter Wagner has been a modern pioneer in studying spiritual gifts and their impact on church growth. While there are points of difference between Dr. Wagner and others on some aspects of gift theology, his basic work has been of unquestionable value. Dr. Wagner lists five steps to take in discovering spiritual gifts (and we have added a sixth). They are:

1. *"Explore the possibilities."* You have been doing this mentally and in conversations with friends while you have gone through the first five chapters of this book. These possibilities have been revealed to you from the pages of Scripture and from the gifted teachers who wrote the chapters.

2. *"Experiment with as many as you can."* You discover spiritual gifts the same way you discover natural tal-

ents—by trying them out. No one ever learned to swim, ride a bicycle, or sing an aria by reading a book. You have to get involved in doing. The same is true of spiritual gifts.

3. *"Examine your feelings."* Do you feel good about yourself as you attempt to exercise that particular gift? If you have strong negative feelings about it, perhaps you should continue to reevaluate.

4. *"Evaluate your effectiveness."* Spiritual gifts are given by God for specific purposes. They will bring results as you exercise them.

5. *"Expect confirmation from the Body."* If you are the only one who thinks you have a gift, you probably don't have that gift. Remember that gifts are given not for your own benefit but for the benefit of the Body. Therefore it is natural that the Body should recognize its benefit.

6. *"Expect an inner confirmation by God's Spirit."* This sixth step was added by Dr. Paul Orjala in *Get Ready to Grow.* We must never allow ourselves to think that the gifts of the Holy Spirit are somehow things that can be manipulated according to the right set of human procedures. The witness of the Spirit is essential to our life in the Spirit.

These six steps will lead in concert to the discovery of your spiritual gifts. Each one alone is not enough. The steps must be taken together and must affirm the same result.

RESPONSIBILITIES OR ROLES

One does not need a sense of spiritual "giftedness" to carry out responsibilities or roles. In the human family a parent must act like a parent even though other parents may be more successful. A true "parent role" requires providing food, shelter, education, and spiritual nurture

97

for children. Children can be very inconvenient! Parents make uncounted adjustments to accommodate to the child's schedules, lessons, and school activities. Many of the responsibilities of parenthood are exercised out of necessity rather than desire.

Christian responsibilities likewise rest on all of us who are committed to Jesus Christ. Paul urged in Rom. 12:3 that we "think soberly" but not too "highly" of ourselves in these matters (KJV). As a Christian, I may *not* have the spiritual gift of giving, which includes ability to earn money, but I am required to be a faithful steward of what I do earn. That means that tithing faithfully is a minimum and a lifelong habit.

Once I belonged to a local church with a church board that did some unwise things (at least in my way of thinking). I did not quit the church, nor did I stop paying my tithe or giving offerings. There are two things to remember about local church leadership: (1) they will sometimes do unwise things (in someone's mind at least); (2) the leadership will eventually change. I take the attitude that my role as a Christian is to help those who have the responsibility and be faithful to my responsibilities in the Body of Christ. Given enough time, prayer, and experience, leadership will usually improve.

Prayer is a responsibility but also a blessed privilege. Saving faith is a prerequisite to entering the kingdom of God, and faith must continually be exercised by Christians. Showing hospitality to those inside and outside the Church is also a Christian's great privilege. You don't have to have a strong sense of spiritual "giftedness" to fulfill these responsibilities.

I once saw a great biblical scholar, Dr. Ralph Earle, do an impromptu unobtrusive cleaning job in a district camp meeting where he was the featured attraction. He simply moved quickly to tidy up a mess before anyone else might observe it. It was not his assignment. He had just come from addressing 1,000 or more people on biblical truths. Something needed to be done quickly for everyone's comfort, and he did it.

It might be profitable to make a list of the many incidents you have observed where responsibilities/roles were fulfilled by those who were not assigned or even "gifted" in that area of responsibility.

Did not Jesus once say, "I am among you as one who serves" (Luke 22:27), and "The greatest among you will be your servant" (Matt. 23:11)?

COUNTERFEITING THE GIFTS

Don't forget that fruit is required of all Christians, but all the gifts are not. We do believe that God gives to every Christian gifts to be developed and deployed for maximum success in the Church. While the fruit of the Spirit cannot be successfully counterfeited, any and all of the gifts can be counterfeited. Who can counterfeit real love or spiritual joy or peace or longsuffering? Those who try to counterfeit fruit are soon discovered.

While spiritual gifts can be counterfeited, it is important to realize that our failure to understand the spiritual gifts does lie at the root of failure to grow in many thousands of churches. Church members are frustrated and guilt-ridden in some cases. Can we find some practical handles to help us all grow better, utilizing spiritual gifts? I sincerely hope so.

DEVELOP GIFTS

In her chapter, Dr. Mildred Wynkoop has emphasized the relationship between natural talent and spiritual gifts. Though they are not the same, they are related. Just as natural talents do not spring full bloom into their mature state at the birth of an infant, so spiritual gifts do not emerge mature and complete at the instant of discovery.

They must be developed in the context of the Body of Christ. I am listing some of the gifts that have already been discussed in this book and have you think with me about ways to develop them for your own portfolio of ministries to the Body.

Prophecy

To some, God gives an unusual ability to communicate His messages to the body of believers for their edification. We usually believe this to be a gift of the assigned pastor. I well remember how hard I worked as a pastor in prayer, in study, in Bible interpretation, to find a Spirit-anointed message to communicate. I now observe as a traveling church executive how keenly conscious our pastors are of this responsibility and how hard they work, often fasting and praying to fulfill God's divine assignments to communicate His message. How fortunate we are to have so many dedicated prophets.

A few years ago our Department of Education and the Ministry discovered in a survey of college and seminary students that there were 2,221 young people enrolled in the Nazarene schools of higher education who felt that God had called them to full-time Christian service, most of them to be pastors, evangelists, missionaries, or Christian teachers. Surely God has been answering the prayers of Nazarenes for God-called workers. This is a force much larger than the minimum requirements for the replacement of pastors, evangelists, and missionaries who die and retire annually. This should be the occasion of great rejoicing for Nazarenes.

We must remember that our schools can only train the material we send from our local churches. So every local church has a responsibility to keep a climate of victory, joy, and growth in the church in order to display good "models" for the young to follow.

In this study however we are not trying to deal with career positions. We have focused on helping lay persons find "their ministry." Is there ever a time where lay persons have the spiritual gift of prophet, and if so, how can this be known?

Most assuredly some lay persons have received a divine call to deliver a prophetic message to the church. Such a voice of prophecy with God's message has strengthened, equipped, motivated, or inspired members of the household of faith.

Teaching

Teaching is akin to preaching. It is communication of the highest order. Like preaching, it is for the edification of the Body. It fills in the biblical message in greater detail, applying it, and personalizing it. Participants have greater opportunity for interacting, explaining and reinforcing the message with fellow believers.

What a pity we have so few teachers. We *could have* many more if only two things happened in local churches.

1. We need to broaden the program base by creating many more places for teachers to teach and by equipping them to do it.

2. We need to rearrange or add to facilities to allow physical space for many newly equipped teachers to teach the unsearchable riches of Christ.

Alternate plans could allow for teaching in homes, in rented halls, restaurants, under the shade of a tree, or wherever people could be gathered. Some churches in congested inner-city areas, as well as in rural towns, have found innovative ways to do both of the above, and churches have greatly grown.

101

We are seriously plateaued in perhaps a thousand places until local leadership decides to "release ministry" to many more teachers and workers. It is easy to build up to 35 members in the local church and not too hard to reach 74 members (57 percent of Nazarene churches had 74 members or less in 1978). It is quite difficult to reach the 125-member level, and only 10 percent of our churches have gone above the 200-member mark.

Ability to move from one plateau upward always revolves around willingness to release ministries to newer and perhaps untried persons. God has given spiritual gifts to all of His children. The Holy Spirit that cleanses also anoints for service. What a pity to see the "old pioneers" (who were there first) frustrate the dynamism of the newer "homesteaders" (the Johny-come-latelys) in trying to exalt Christ through use of spiritual gifts in the church.

It seems costly to give up some turf and prepare newer talent for sharing leadership, but if done in the Spirit and with proper preparation, it pays greatly in expansion of Christ's kingdom. New souls are won and the work grows and multiplies.

DEVELOPMENT OF PROPHETS AND TEACHERS

You don't need to wait for a classroom and an official assignment to exercise your spiritual gift of prophet or teacher. Here are practical steps to take right now.

1. *Be faithful to the means of grace*—in prayer, in Bible study, and in attendance. Practice good stewardship of tithing money and time. Keep a good spirit.

2. *Practice relating biblical principles to life situations* (such as the news and passing events).

3. *Observe those who explain the Word of God,* such as your pastor or your Sunday school teacher. How do they

do it? Is there a consistent pattern in their teaching? Are they successfully communicating? If not, why not? You can learn from their failures as well as their successes. The failure to successfully communicate can teach you more sometimes than the always "successful" methodology.

4. *Find someone you can teach.* It may be one of your children or a neighbor's boy or girl. It may be a backyard Bible class or a home Bible study. It might be at Sunday school or it might be teaching a friend. That friend doesn't even need to know that he or she is being taught. You will know what you are trying to teach from the Word of God, and you will observe it take root in someone else's life. Preachers do this all the time when they prayerfully select scripture to be read when visiting in homes or at hospital bedsides. Often the message must be gently and subtly introduced into the conscious mind of the learner target. The best teaching may be the unobtrusive, gentle illustration or testimony.

5. *Study teaching methods.* Learn from denominational quarterlies and teaching aids. Be willing to respond to requests from local church leaders to assist in teaching a class. Immerse yourself in a teaching environment. Be a learner yourself; active learners make the best teachers. Contact the Division of Christian Life and the Christian Service Training office for suggestions (6401 The Paseo, Kansas City, MO 64131).

By all means develop the young through utilizing talents, skills, and abilities. Frequently we discover young men studying for the ministry who never taught a Sunday school class. Who is responsible for that condition? You can blame the young man if you like, but I believe the fault lies with a church that is too self-centered, too preoccupied with not disturbing the old pioneers to allow for development of the young who are being brought in through the front door, sometimes in large numbers. What good is it to bring in masses of young people if we only allow them to exit without discipling and deploying them in the Master's harvest?

I have gone to extra pains sometimes to slip into a class to study the methods of the teacher. I have observed that the most successful communicators didn't do all the talking all the time. They allowed others to speak and to give reaction. They prepared others to present material. They seemed to direct the thoughts of the class to the basic principles. They put everyone at ease. They displayed a fellow feeling for each one who participated without putting anybody down. They seemed to identify with and understand the problems of the young and the old. Their concern registered. Their styles were intellectually stimulating, thought provoking. People should feel helped at the end of every session.

Serving

My wife, Madelyn, and I compared notes and agreed that one of the finest examples of serving that we had witnessed recently was Mrs. Fred Stephens in Greystones, County Wicklow, near Dublin, Ireland. One Sunday we saw her stretch a dining room table that would ordinarily seat 6 out to a table for 20. She did it humbly and smoothly, so beautifully and with such warmth. She does this often, as you might guess. We observed also the same meek, humble, effective manner when helping to entertain 150 North Irish folks in a YMCA hall in the heart of Dublin. She had first-class assistance from her husband and a half dozen members of our Dublin fellowship.

The 150 from North Ireland came from our churches there to welcome pioneer Superintendent Harold and Vera Brown, but also to affirm and support by their presence and interest the small group that makes up our house church in Dublin. Mrs. Stephens was behind the scenes, seldom verbal in expressing herself, but hard at work making sandwiches and arranging other goodies for the guests. Sunday morning in her quiet, meek, unobtrusive manner, she led the children to another room so that the 30 adults could worship in the small apartment living room.

We have a Nazarene neighbor who is like that. She is meek, unassuming. Recently she volunteered to take two little children two days per week to help a neighbor who was recently divorced. Our neighbors go to her on a regular basis for advice and spiritual counsel.

Jesus said that "the meek . . . will inherit the earth" (Matt. 5:5). All prophets and teachers, take note that in Romans Paul put serving in between prophecy and teaching and followed teaching with the gift of encouragement.

In developing your possibilities in the gift of serving, make a specific effort to think of the things you can do for other members of the Body. Watch for ways to serve. Open the door for someone with his hands full, share your hymnal (be sure the hymnal is open to the right page). Giving cups of cold water and helping the helpless may seem passé, but how often do we utilize creative means to serve? We are great on doing this for people who are far away, but what about those near at hand?

Hospitality/Helps

It is evident in the explanation of the gift of serving that we have included characteristics that relate to the gift of hospitality and the gift of helps. Can you differentiate between the three gifts?

Hospitality. Dr. C. Peter Wagner defines the gift of hospitality as the "love of strangers."[1] Those with this gift have the special ability to create an open, accepting, and warm atmosphere around those in need. A bonding of hearts occurs through their generous hospitality. These people are happiest when their homes are full and they are meeting the needs of their guests. The satisfaction of the visitor's needs is of primary importance. Wagner writes, "The motto of a person with this gift is 'hospitality before pride.'"[2] Everything does not have to be in perfect order before a guest is welcomed into the home; that individual's need is more important than what the breakfast dishes look like stacked in the sink or the newspaper strewn about the living room floor.

Helps. Whereas the gift of serving is directed more toward a group or institution, the gift of hospitality and the gift of helps are done on a one-to-one basis. And, whereas the gift of hospitality is directed toward anyone in need, the gift of helps is geared toward the Christian individual.

Wagner defines the gift of helps as the God-given ability "to invest talents in the life and ministry of other members of the Body, thus enabling the person helped to increase the effectiveness of his or her spiritual gifts."[3]

It is my privilege to serve as executive director of a highly diversified department. We deal with new districts, language churches, ethnic minority churches, church architecture, home mission church loans, organizations of new churches, missionary reading and study materials, church growth materials, inner-city work, training seminars, experimental ministries, and a $2 million budget including Alabaster, minority ministerial student scholarships, and much more. For these areas I have many fine helpers. Harold Allen, administrative assistant; John Oster, editor; Franklin Cook, coordinator of Urban Missions; and Jan, Kathy, Linda, Cecilia, Mary, Cheryl, Charles, Dale, Gladys, and Arlene all are great helpers to me. They think creatively with me, enlarging my influence in every activity. They are every bit as important in God's eyes as the executive.

Who are the helpers in your church? What would happen (or fail to happen) if your church suddenly lost these "gifted" persons?

Encouraging

Encouraging or exhorting means offering words of strength and help to members of the Body for their edification. This can be on a person-to-person basis or in groups. It usually is one on one. Pray for someone lonely or discouraged; select someone specifically each day and do or say something to encourage that person; make a checklist of new members, forgotten ones—the possible candidates for loneliness; take flowers to shut-ins; ask the budding photographer or musician to demonstrate his or her specialty. Watch for the little physical signs that tell you someone is discouraged, and carry out a deliberate strategy to see that person's spirits lifted.

My office assistant, Gladys Johnson, has made a career of using her spiritual gift of encouragement during the 11 years of employment in the Department of Home Missions. She even signs her memos "Glad." I'm glad she's around. She is a constant encouragement. She left a business career at considerable inconvenience and sacrifice to serve the church and is typical of many of our headquarters workers.

You can develop this gift by placing circles of love and understanding around those recently bereaved or divorced or jobless, or those passing through a major crisis in life.

Giving

For every 1 with the spiritual gift of giving, there must be 1,000 who do not have this gift but are faithful stewards in giving tithes and offerings. The special gift of giving always depends on the ability to earn. A favorite trick of the devil is to get God's people to seek spiritual gifts. Those who are foolish enough to seek gifts become frustrated if not spiritually destitute. Some are deluded into unwise and radical acts of giving, hoping that the commitment would make them "wealthy" givers.

As a pastor I preached at regular intervals on stewardship themes. A retired, destitute, but faithful widow confessed to great discouragement because she could not give much money. Well known and loved by us all, she had practically no income and merely existed (physically at least). She said, "I have no income of any kind."

I probed as gently as I could. "How much is 10 percent of zero?" She saw the point and smiled when I added, "If God has entrusted you with zero income, the tithe of the increase is zero, and that is as important to God as the tithe of $1 million." You see, God wants us, all that we are and have, whether it is little or much.

Some superslick, success-oriented persons have always been around to make the gullible believe in "giving greatly in order to *get* greatly." It just doesn't work that way. Some of God's children do have talent for making much money, and we thank God for them. They make possible enormous assets to further God's work. I know some of these spiritual and financial giants in Texas, Oregon, Ireland, New England, Colorado, Kansas, Missouri, Oklahoma, California, Illinois, Ohio, Canada, and many, many other places. They really do have the gift of getting money and of giving it.

But what about little old me? Aren't we all supposed to experiment with gifts? Certainly! And this could be the most fun of all as we experiment with the gift of giving. Mr. John Oster, editor in the Department of Home Missions, is always so creative and helpful to me in many different ways. He has suggested the following.

For once, give a gift you don't have to give. Try giving

anonymously. See the difference it makes in people's lives and in your own life. Set a giving goal above your established tithe for a specific period. See how it makes you feel. See if it makes the difference in the Body achieving some financial goal. Seek inventive ways to give; don't always give money. Give clothes, or food, or time, or whatever is needed and appropriate. Give daringly and examine your feelings. Is God with you when you give?

(To stimulate the whole church in the area of experimenting with this gift, I strongly urge that you see the new film produced by the Department of Stewardship, *The Gift of Love*. You can order it from the Nazarene Publishing House.)

Leadership

I like the definition of leadership given by C. Peter Wagner in his new book on spiritual gifts. He says,

> The gift of leadership is the special ability that God gives to certain members of the Body of Christ to set goals in accordance with God's purpose for the future and to communicate these goals to others in such a way that they voluntarily and harmoniously work together to accomplish those goals for the glory of God.[4]

A leader is a leader to the extent he or she has a following. That is a truism. Church folks are more loyal and sensitive to church leaders than the rank and file in secular organizations. That is because the Body of Christ is knit together in such strong ties of love and mutual support. This often makes us blind to our faults and gullible about poor methods. We often assume we are doing better than the facts reveal.

Every Christian should be optimistic and full of faith about the gospel, but good leaders must also be pragmatic. That means they should get all of the data, be honest about programs that aren't working and get rid of them, and develop methods that do work.

Leadership is especially charged with the responsibility of observing the harvest, finding responsive areas, and training and deploying workers to reach the goal of making disciples.

Leadership is something, however, that everyone should experiment with to a greater or lesser degree. Why not do some of that experimenting now? Here are some suggestions.

Observe what needs to be done around the church. Test your leadership; do something about it. Will others follow your lead? You will never know until you try. Leaders must have courage. You will have to stand out a little from the rest or they will not be able to follow you. Test your leadership in smaller things before you try a major project. There are lots of little things you can notice that would be taken care of with a little leadership from you. Always be faithful if you wish to gain the necessary respect from those who would follow your leadership.

Mercy

Sure, you're kind, but who knows that besides you? Seek ways to demonstrate kindness. Find out about those in the Body who are ill or in distress. Look within yourself to discover what you would feel like in a similar circumstance. What would make things better? Do that for the other person. Deliberately set out to demonstrate mercy. Picture Jesus walking in your shoes. Would He find any opportunities to be merciful? Perhaps the Holy Spirit will lead you in some act of mercy.

Evangelist

Unless you already have some idea that this is your gift, don't begin with this one. Practice some of the other gifts first. They will open the doors of witnessing opportunities for you. Then experiment with the gift of evangelism. This is the God-given grace to lead another soul to Christ. Familiarize yourself with salvation scriptures and some specific witnessing plans such as those developed by our Department of Evangelism.

We all know that every born-again Christian should witness, or should be willing, able, and ready to witness. Careful studies reveal that very little witnessing is being done. The worker analysis borrowed from the *Diagnostic Clinic* (see Appendix B) will surprise most church leaders in its revelation of how few are engaged in outreach. Many members have the gift of evangelist. This gift is a reproductive function. We need to discover who they are, train them, and deploy them in this important assignment.

I recently assisted a church of 600 members to analyze its workers, and we discovered about 1.5 percent of the total church membership was employed in direct outreach. It is obvious that this great church needs to redeploy large numbers of its membership into outreach activities even if it means pulling them out of maintenance-type jobs to accomplish this.

Usually not more than 10 percent of the total membership in strong evangelistic churches are engaged in outreach activities. Most of the member-power of a local congregation is involved with ushering, teaching, singing, cleaning, administering, etc. The maintenance-type jobs that perpetuate the institution take almost all the energy of the local church.

How does your church rate in the percentage of the membership directly involved in weekly personal evangelism efforts, and weekly visitation to find new attenders or prospects?

It is important for the church to experience internal growth as well as expansion growth. A good goal for your church is to involve 50 percent of all of the members in some kind of maintenance responsibility such as instruction or ministry. Then, if you are able to get more than 10 percent of your membership involved in weekly evangelistic pursuits of outreach, you will most assuredly have good growth.

Missionary

The missionary gift is definitely cross-cultural. Deliberately associate yourself with cultural groups other than your own in witnessing and serving situations. Explore your ability to learn another language. Teach an ethnic minority Sunday school class. Examine your effectiveness in witnessing across cultural barriers. Volunteer to do mission work in the inner city. Bring a person or family of a different race or socioeconomic group into your home for Sunday dinner and an afternoon of visiting, singing, explaining scriptures, and sharing spiritual insights. Call the Chamber of Commerce or school board office to learn how many racial minorities there are in your community and where they are located. Discover their needs.

Wisdom

What does the Bible really have to say about the way we live? What does it say about the solutions to the problems of the family, the church, the community, the state, the nation, the world? The Bible says that, if we ask for it, wisdom is available. "If any of you lacks wisdom, he should ask God, who gives generously to all without finding fault, and it will be given to him" (Jas. 1:5). Examine the Scripture specifically to find what it says about problem solving. Discuss your understanding of biblical solutions with other Christians, including your teachers and your pastor. Test it against the experience of older Christians in the faith. Try out your understandings in little things as you build confidence in your ability to exercise the gift of wisdom. Don't rush ahead of the light that God has given you, but do seek and apply wisdom. You need all you can get; we all do.

Pastor/Shepherd

Early in this course you may have filled out a spiritual gifts profile; if you did, you no doubt discovered that you had a high score on pastor/shepherd. This may have surprised you. The pastor/shepherd is the best-known model for full-time clergy in most denominations. We have been taught that each congregation has a pastor-shepherd. He cares for the sheep, feeds them, and responds to their hurts and their needs. He assumes responsibility for their spiritual well-being, putting their needs and welfare above all other concerns. He often beats the doctor to the home where there is serious and sudden illness. He stands by the family in time of death and discouragement. He advises, counsels, and in many ways contributes to the spiritual, social, physical, and even economic well-being of those for whom he has shepherding responsibilities.

We have discovered also that laypersons often have the spiritual gift of pastor/shepherd. If you rated a high score on "pastor," on the spiritual gifts profile, that does not necessarily mean you are supposed to leave your job and place in the community and go away to study for the full-time ministry. This simple test may have alerted some to what God is calling them to do as a lifetime assignment. But don't assume that this simple test indicates God's long-term will for everyone's life as a full-time clergyman. You may be an effective shepherd as a layperson.

The liabilities of the pastor/shepherd model in the usually accepted sense is that one shepherd can minister to only a few people. He may not be able to minister to more than 40 or 50 persons on a first- and last-name basis. If he has 100 families in his congregation, the pastor/shepherd

113

will be literally working night and day in an effort to minister to them as the shepherd. This explains why most churches plateau before they get 100 adult members. It is physically impossible for one shepherd (especially if he feels impelled to do all of the shepherding) to minister to a congregation of more than 100 adult members.

The usual answer at this point is to make a strong case for further paid staff. In fact, a paid staff is quite a status symbol. The more people you have under you, the more important you are supposed to be according to the philosophy based on the American success syndrome. We affirm that a paid staff can be extremely important when judiciously incorported into a pastor team. In fact, there are few great churches of many hundreds or thousands of members that do not have a highly competent paid staff.

No matter what size church, the paid staff can only do so much shepherding. What we need in every church are many people with the spiritual gift of pastor/shepherd, who are willing to take long-term spiritual responsibility for 15 or 20 adults and their family members to provide spiritual nurture and pastoral care.

Recently I had lunch with Mr. and Mrs. Wilbert Eichenberger from the Garden Grove Community Church in California and learned that they have 529 lay ministers of pastoral care who attend to the shepherding work of this church of 9,000 members. These lay ministers serve under the general leadership and supervision of a paid staff member.

This is what finding your ministry is all about for large numbers, because most pastoral leaders have a problem in releasing part of "their" ministry to undershepherds, and most laypersons look upon the pastor as a hired hand who is paid to do the pastoral shepherding. And that is the main reason so many churches are plateaued in their

114

growth. We must find some way to get 2,600 churches that have 74 members or less to multiply their ministry in some way. The best method is to set apart laypersons who have spiritual gifts in shepherding to shepherd small groups of people within the church.

If 1 out of every 10 adult church members were assigned the pastoral care of 10 other families, the pastoral leader could maximize his time and ministry and the church would grow. These undershepherds could check every Sunday to see if all members of their groups were in all of the services. If one were absent, a telephone call or personal visit on Sunday would discover if there was sickness, death, or other problems. Information about each individual could be fed into the church office where other appropriate follow-up action could on occasion be taken. Each member needs to be made to feel that he or she is a part of a caring, loving fellowship.

We have lots of business persons who travel in their business. An undershepherd could follow them by prayer and contact on extended trips and make them feel a part of the fellowship though their work took them far away. Birthdays and anniversaries could be remembered with a simple card of greeting. Spiritual problems could be dealt with in concert with the pastor. There is no doubt in my mind but that we could double the membership in 2,500 churches in a very short time if we were dedicated enough and loving enough to commit ourselves to releasing ministry to many undershepherds in the church.

The weekly checklist could include the absent, spiritual needs, emergencies, illnesses, and changes in work, such as retirements, layoffs, promotions, and so forth. Every undershepherd could be at the church early on Sunday morning filled with anticipation to help members of his flock out of their cars and into the church, keeping spare umbrellas for rainy seasons, helping the aged and infirm, creating a great spirit of joyful excitement in the atmosphere.

Many have the shepherding qualities though not chosen to teach a Bible class or lead a choir. Their ministry is needed. Church members have a sense of belonging to an extended family. They want to feel loved, appreciated, missed. For a more carefully documented plan of utilizing undershepherds, see Dr. Millard Reed's excellent little book, *Let Your Church Grow,* which can be ordered from the Nazarene Publishing House.

DEPLOYMENT OF SPIRITUAL GIFTS

What I have given here is just a sample. Apply the same type of thinking to any proposed gift that you think you might have. Now would be a good time to make a list of spiritual gifts operative in your local church that we have not written about in this brief text. Who has this gift? How is it being used?

Of course you have made a start toward deploying gifts by experimenting with as many as you can in order to discover what gifts you have. You have gone a little bit farther down the road of deployment as you have developed the gifts that you have been able to recognize within you.

The deployment of your spiritual gifts will come in concert with others in the Body of Christ so that the specific needs of the Body are met. The needs in one local church may be slightly different than in another. The gift mix of one church or even one denomination may be different from another. The deployment of your spiritual gifts will always be for the good of the entire Body and not for your personal well-being although you will receive your maximum benefit by being of maximum service to the Body of which you are a part. The health of the entire Body extends to every part of it.

116

The benefits of developing spiritual gifts are numerous. Here are a few of them:

BENEFITS TO THE CHURCH

1. Each member of the body works together in greater understanding and harmony as each develops his/her gifts.

2. The whole church demonstrates greater love as it learns to share more openly and in patient understanding of each other.

3. Everyone knows his/her own spiritual job description. We do not need to beg or harangue the congregation to volunteer.

4. False humility is eliminated. We learn to admit freely that God has given each of us a special endowment of grace.

5. The whole body matures. There is internal growth of spirit, understanding, love, and knowledge of God's Word and each other.

6. The church grows more and more as the body functions in healthy exercise of its gifts.

7. Souls are saved and disciples made as we let new people or different kinds of people into our loving fellowship.

8. A sensitivity to spiritual options develops. It is normal for us to show concern for all in the employment of our spiritual gifts, not just those like us or who think like us.

BENEFITS TO ME AS AN INDIVIDUAL

1. I will know God's will for my service. I will know my own spiritual job description.

2. I will be freed from unnecessary guilt in being released from thinking I must strive to be something for which I am not divinely endowed.

3. I will be more effective as a servant of Christ because I will feel better about myself and my brothers and sisters in Christ.

4. I will be able to concentrate on developing God's special gift to me instead of wasting time on a less productive effort.

5. I will be able to organize my time for maximum service to God, concentrating on what God has especially endowed me to do.

You will notice that in this final chapter we have not dealt with any of the language and sign gifts. In the previous chapters our scholars have given us excellent biblical exegesis regarding these matters. We see little profit in discussing them, especially in a short introductory course.* The Church of the Nazarene does not believe that speaking in unknown tongues is relevant to the development of our spiritual life and practice. We do not quarrel with those who embrace this teaching; we simply do not include this in our philosophy of ministry or in our mission. We do not believe that any physical sign is necessary to the reception of the Holy Spirit in His sanctifying fullness. We believe the language and sign gifts in general to be nonproductive and even divisive in carrying out the Great Commission of our Lord to disciple the nations.

We have earlier stated that the gifts may be counterfeited. Our long-term interest is upon having the *"fruit* of the Spirit."

---

*For a more complete workshop presentation on spiritual gifts, obtain the *Spiritual Gifts Workshop* by Raymond W. Hurn from the Nazarene Publishing House. It comes complete with a notebook of lecture material that develops scriptural basis in depth on all of the spiritual gifts and includes 10 extra Participant Workbooks that can be filled out by the participants as the lectures are given.

All those who write on the subject of spiritual gifts are quick to point out that some abuses do arise in a congregation as they dwell at length on spiritual gifts. These abuses may arise out of an overemphasis or a distorted emphasis on spiritual gifts, but are likely to surface anyway in some churches. You should be on guard against falling prey to certain abuses.

Gift Exaltation

Dr. C. Peter Wagner sees one common abuse as "gift exaltation."[5] This occurs when undue emphasis and importance is placed on a certain gift. This involves a ranking and rating system of the gifts. Some people will be inclined to look on their gift as being in the upper echelon of spirituality. Other gifts will be treated as being in a lesser position. This distortion occurs when a congregation tries to name the greatest gift. When this happens, the individual is glorified rather than God, the Body gains nothing, and gifts become a means to an end of spiritual status.

Gift Projection

Wagner recognizes another abuse as "gift projection."[6] The problem of gift projection occurs when people fail to see the reason behind their outstanding spiritual accomplishments. They erroneously believe the reason for their victories is because of their ardent love and devotion to God. Therefore, they assume that anyone can duplicate the same, given enough faith, love, devotion, and so on. Consequently, guilt is projected to many Christians. Those without that particular gift are made to feel inadequate and inferior. What these "gift projectors" fail to realize is that the reason they can do what they do is because of the specific *gifts* and *abilities* God has given them, and with those particular gifts they are able to accomplish great spiritual feats. It is not solely because of their great devotion and love for God. We are only responsible for the development and practice of our individual spiritual gift or gifts.

It takes each individual part to make a body. We cannot all be hands or feet—some of us must be eyelids and elbows. You are responsible for your duties as an elbow. You must function properly in order for the upper and lower arm to work at maximum capacity.

Gift Neglect

We cannot neglect our spiritual gift because of fear, inferiority, or laziness. This is one of the greatest abuses. God has given you a spiritual gift or perhaps several gifts for a reason. He has equipped you with the necessary tools to perform the job only you can do.

Your heart is a muscle. To neglect benefiting exercise to build it up damages the whole body. Your body is a muscle to be developed, kept in tune for normal longevity. Your spiritual gift, if not used, becomes like an unused appendage. It shrivels, and in doing so, the whole body is damaged.

In his book *The Gifts of the Spirit,* W. T. Purkiser summarizes well:

> All spiritual gifts are for one purpose—to build the Body. In this sense, all are equal. "Now to each man the manifestation of the Spirit is given for the common good" (1 Corinthians 12:7).[7]

BENEFITS OUTWEIGH ABUSES

Among the remarkable stories of spiritual life and development I have obtained from the Department of Evangelism I find this brief testimony of Mrs. Sarah

Castle to be typical of a great host of those who have developed their evangelist gift.

After several years of married life devoted to materialistic values, she and her husband were won to Christ by the personal evangelism of Wayne Sharpes. Spiritual development was slow at first, though positive. Customers in the beauty shop where she worked noticed the great change and frequently asked questions. Quite a few folks were influenced to visit her church. Then she was invited to take personal evangelism training. Reluctant at first, she began to learn how to be a personal evangelist. Mr. Castle also came to the training and began to share with people at his work. He was satisfied to do the class work but not to go into peoples' homes. He was a good witness in his secular job.

Then one night the team was short a worker and he went along with his wife to help out. It was apparent that God had anointed these two, and souls were being saved. It was so exciting that this husband and wife team went out three nights a week all summer long. Sunday morning and Sunday night they were at the church to welcome the new converts. On Wednesday nights they prayed for the new Christians and took them along to prayer meetings.

One night they were assigned to visit a family they recognized as old drinking buddies they had not seen in four years. It was a tough internal battle. They really didn't want to go. How could these people ever be interested in the gospel of Christ? But they went anyway, and to their surprise they discovered that the Holy Spirit had been working, especially with the husband who had been listening to Billy Graham and each time had prayed with Billy at his TV set. Soon these friends were gloriously saved.

That night of witnessing was the beginning of some wonderful things. The pastor and other Christian friends surrounded the new converts with love and care. Since that night, four years ago, these new Christians, won by the Castles, have been responsible for more than 40 people who have been saved in their homes or through personal witnessing.

The Castles now teach a class for new converts and are both active in follow-up work with new converts. How many Sarah Castles do you suppose we have among us in every church? It really would be like a giant Christmas celebration if we could find a way to unwrap our spiritual gifts and put them to work under the anointing of the Holy Spirit to build the kingdom of Christ.

DISCUSSION QUESTIONS

1. In what way do members fulfill local church roles or responsibilities.

2. How would you develop an innovative plan to double the number of teachers through recruitment, training, and deployment of high school and college-age young people?

3. In what additional ways can we communicate to children and youth a sense of commitment to the Great Commission?

4. Who are the best examples of those with gifts of serving and hospitality in your church? After making a list, answer the question "On what date did I express appreciation to these persons?"

5. Make a list of the different ways leadership gifts need now to be exercised in your church. What can you and others do to affirm young people who appear to have a gift of leadership?

6. Discuss the lay persons who have the gift of shepherding. How can undershepherds release your pastor to train personal evangelists and concentrate on getting new people into your church? What tensions will this cause? How can you anticipate these and prepare people in advance to release your pastor from doing all the shepherding?

7. Discuss how more lay persons can be trained and deployed in personal evangelism. What were the important moments of decision in the life of Mr. and Mrs. Castle?

For Additional Reading

Dudley, Carl S. *Making the Small Church Effective.* Nashville: Abingdon Press, 1978.

MacNair, Donald J. *The Birth, Care, and Feeding of a Local Church.* Grand Rapids: Baker Book House, 1971.

McGavran, Donald A.; and Arn, Winfield C. *Ten Steps for Church Growth.* San Francisco: Harper and Row, Publishers, 1977.

Rich, Marion K. *Discovery: The Art of Leading Small Groups.* Kansas City: Beacon Hill Press of Kansas City, 1978.

Schaller, Lyle E. *The Decision-Makers.* Nashville: Abingdon Press, 1974.

Shanafelt, Ira L. *The Evangelical Home Bible Class.* Kansas City: Beacon Hill Press of Kansas City, 1969.

Wiseman, Neil B. *Leadership.* Kansas City: Beacon Hill Press of Kansas City, 1979.

Appendix A

1. Prophecy
2. Serving
3. Helping
4. Teaching
5. Encouraging
6. Giving
7. Leadership
8. Mercy/Compassion
9. Pastor/Shepherd
10. Apostle
11. Missionary
12. Evangelist
13. Wisdom
14. Knowledge
15. Discernment of Spirits
16. Healing
17. Miracles
18. Faith
19. Languages
20. Interpretation of Languages

Note: Young people in most churches will have some problems with questions that focus on local church involvement (i.e., ". . . people have told me," etc.). This is due to our failure to disciple and deploy the young. Young adults out of college may also have a struggle here.

Appendix B

Let's find out what kind of work is done by our church. Listed below are the kinds of work normally done by the church. If applicable to your church, put a check mark (✔) to show whether each kind of work is directed toward churched or unchurched people.

Kind of Work	Churched	Unchurched
1. Teaching Sunday School	✓	
2. Keeping Records	✓	
3. Superintending/Supervising	✓	
4. Board/Committee Planning		
5. Weekly Personal Soul Winning		
6. Ushering	✓	
7. Overseeing Ushers	✓	
8. Choir Rehearsal and Singing	✓	
9. Music Coordinating and Leading	✓	
10. Accompanying Choir/Congregation	✓	
11. Leading Home Bible Studies		
12. Hosting Home Bible Studies		
13. Hospital Visitation	✓	
14. Home Visitation	✓	
15. Nursery Care Work	✓	
16. Benevolent and Social Work	✓	
17. Children's Work	✓	
18. Youth Work	✓	
19. Committee Work	✓	
Other:		
20. _____		

21.	_____	_____	_____
22.	_____	_____	_____
23.	_____	_____	_____
24.	_____	_____	_____
	Totals	_____	_____

Class 1 Workers
(Those unpaid workers who serve the existing
church body in maintenance-type work)

Tabulate the number of each kind of Class 1 workers in your church. There is much overlap in churches in that many people wear more than one hat, but the starting place in measuring your work force ought to be the number of people in any position; then you can refine by eliminating overlap.

First indicate the number of workers in each category (see example). Then estimate the average number of hours spent weekly in the actual doing and/or preparation of the job for each worker in each category. For instance: committee work and preparing for committee meetings, etc. Now multiply Column 1 by Column 2 to determine the total hours invested weekly in doing this task in the church. Finally, add up all three columns.

Kinds of *Class 1 Workers*	*1* *Total* *Number* *Workers*	*2* *Average* *Hours* *Worked* *Per* *Week*	*3* *Total* *Hours* *Worked* *Per* *Week*
Example:			
Teachers for Sunday School	50 ×	8 =	400
1. Teachers for Sunday School	_____	_____	_____
2. Christian Life Leaders	_____	_____	_____
3. Record Keepers	_____	_____	_____

126

4. Church Board Members			
5. Leaders of Home Bible Studies			
6. Follow-up of Moving Nazarenes			
7. Promotion, Publicity			
8. Librarians			
9. Ushers			
10. Choir Director/Instrumentalists			
11. Choir Singers			
12. Nursery Attendants			
13. Hospital Visitation Workers			
14. Children's Workers			
15. Youth Workers			
16. Young Adult Workers			
17. Committee Members			

Other:

18. _____
19. _____
20. _____

Totals

CLASS 2 WORKERS

Class 2 represents volunteer (unpaid) workers who head out away from the church. They actively reach out to others in the community who need Christ. They may do the work in the community or at the church site, but their focus is always on the unchurched. This class worker may be involved in weekly personal evangelism, canvassing for new prospects, follow-up of new contacts, etc. They usually work to see people converted or work to meet human needs (i.e., social concerns, reconciliation, etc.).

Following the same procedure as you did with Class 1 workers, now calculate the totals for Class 2 workers in each column.

Kinds of *Class 2 Workers*	*1* *Total* *Number* *Workers*	*2* *Average* *Hours* *Worked* *Per* *Week*	*3* *Total* *Hours* *Worked* *Per* *Week*
Example:			
Weekly Personal Evangelism	5	× 10	= 50
1. Weekly Personal Evangelism			
2. Canvassing for New Prospects			
3. Follow-up of New Prospects			
4. _____			
5. _____			
6. Meeting Human Needs in Social Concerns, Reconciliation, Etc.			
Totals			

Unpaid Worker Balance

Put the total number of Class 1 and Class 2 workers and total hours worked per week in the respective boxes below. Compare with total church members.

Our church membership is _____.

Class 1 Workers Total
(Those who serve the existing church body)

Total Class 1 Workers   *Total Hours Worked Each Week*

_____% of total church membership

Class 2 Workers Total
(Those who head outward from the church in outreach)

Total Class 2 Workers   *Total Hours Worked Each Week*

_____% of total church membership

SUMMARY

Show percentage of membership that is Class 1, Class 2, and the remaining percent that are consumers.

Class 1 Workers   *Class 2 Workers*   *Consumers*

%   %   %

How does your worker balance compare with the churches on the chart?

The Worker Analysis (Appendix B) is modified from the *Diagnostic Clinic* published by the Nazarene Publishing House and developed by Fuller Evangelistic Association. Used by permission.

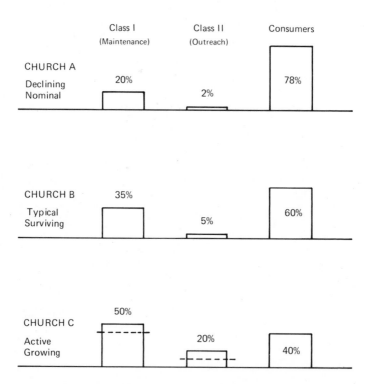

	Class I (Maintenance)	Class II (Outreach)	Consumers
CHURCH A Declining Nominal	20%	2%	78%
CHURCH B Typical Surviving	35%	5%	60%
CHURCH C Active Growing	50%	20%	40%

Note: In Church C there may be an overlap of as much as 10 percent in Class 1 and Class 2 workers (i.e., Sunday school teachers who also spend time weekly in personal soul winning).

Modified from Dr. Donald McGavran's "Classes of Workers"

Reference Notes

Chapter 1:

1. William M. Greathouse, *From the Apostles to Wesley* (Kansas City, Mo.: Beacon Hill Press of Kansas City, 1979).

2. W. T. Purkiser, *The Gifts of the Spirit* (Kansas City, Mo.: Beacon Hill Press of Kansas City, 1975), p. 16.

3. *Ibid.,* pp. 16-17.

4. C. Peter Wagner, *Your Spiritual Gifts Can Help Your Church Grow* (Glendale, Calif.: Regal Books, 1979), p. 32.

Chapter 4:

1. William F. Orr and James Arthur Walter, *1 Corinthians* (New York: Doubleday & Co., Inc., 1976), p. 282.

Chapter 5:

1. Purkiser, *The Gifts of the Spirit,* p. 26.

Chapter 6:

1. C. Peter Wagner, *Your Spiritual Gifts Can Help Your Church Grow,* p. 70.

2. *Ibid.*

3. *Ibid.,* p. 262.

4. *Ibid.,* p. 260.

5. *Ibid.,* p. 53.

6. *Ibid.*

7. Purkiser, *The Gifts of the Spirit,* p. 22.